The Surprising Health Benefits of Whiskey and Cigars

The Surprising Health Benefits of Whiskey and Cigars

A Love Letter to the Lifestyle, Science, and Simple

Pleasures of Two Timeless Indulgences

By Earl M. McCune

Foreword

    This book is dedicated to my friends at Smokers Etc., the heart and soul of Stow, Ohio. Around our humble circle of chairs and in that single walk-in humidor, you taught me that camaraderie is as rich as any cigar and that a shared pour can mend even the longest day. Thank you for your laughter, for the debates that drifted into the night, and for the family you've given me. This book is for you—brothers and sisters of the leaf, bourbon lovers, and all who know that life is best savored slowly.

Contents

CHAPTER 1

The Timeless Allure of Whiskey and Cigars

There are very few things in life that carry the same weight of tradition, ritual, and plain enjoyment as whiskey and

cigars. They are timeless not because they never change, but because their purpose has never needed an update. Both have walked beside history—from palaces and parliament chambers to front porches and small-town lounges. They invite us to slow down, pay attention, and feel time again. If the modern world is a fast river, whiskey and cigars are a quiet bend on the bank where you can sit and hear yourself think. To pour a glass properly, you do it with your whole hand, not your phone hand. You set the distractions aside. The bottle tips and the amber slips into the glass like a sunrise arriving on schedule. You hold a cigar near your nose and breathe in the barn, the cedar, the dried fruit, and the promise of warmth. Nothing has happened yet—no sip, no puff —and already the moment has more weight. This is the first magic of the pairing:

anticipation elevated to a ritual. The second magic is patience. Nothing about the experience is efficient, and that is the point. A good cigar refuses to be rushed; it will burn at its own speed or it will punish you with a hot, bitter lesson. A proper whiskey opens in stages: shy at first, then generous as oxygen loosens its tongue. In a world that sells speed as the only virtue, these two are quiet mentors reminding us that unhurried work still has a place in a life well lived. If you listen while you light, you can hear tobacco crackle softly as flame meets leaf. The foot blooms orange, then settles into a steady glow. Your first puffs are more ceremony than smoke: you are coaxing, not conquering. The draw steadies. The burn line steadies. You roll the glass, watch the legs, and catch that first nose full of oak, vanilla, citrus, or spice—the chorus depending on the bottle. This is not a test. It is an introduction between old friends. The pairing is older than fashion and younger than boredom. Whiskey began as a way to save grain from spoilage and to carry value down muddy roads without a wagon full of sacks. Tobacco began as a leaf with sacred meaning —a plant people believed connected earth to sky. Neither origin story mentions hustle. They speak of patience and care—of farmers who watch the weather, coopers who choose wood wisely, blenders who listen to barrels, and torcedores who train their hands until a line of leaf sits like a seam of silk. If you pull back the curtain and look at the work behind the romance, the allure deepens. The barley or corn or rye is planted, watered, cut, and malted. It is milled and mashed; sugar becomes wort; quiet yeast changes sweet liquid to young fire. Copper stills sing. The spirit rests in oak that was once a living tree reaching for light. Years pass while the angels take their share. A distiller can no more hurry a barrel than a farmer can scold the moon into rising early. On the cigar side, seed becomes seedling and seedling becomes broad leaf. The plants reach for Caribbean sun or climb cool hills in Central America.

Harvest is hands and knives and careful stacks. Leaves are hung in barns and learn to breathe slowly. They ferment in pilones, warm from their own transformation, watched and turned so they do not scorch. After months and sometimes years, the tobacco is finally calm enough to be rolled. Someone sits with a chaveta and a cutting board and turns a handful of dried leaves into an hour's peace. Maybe the deepest common note between whiskey and cigars is workmanship. Even the simplest bottle and the humblest stick were touched by people who cared how they turned out. That care is what you taste. We can pretend we are only after flavor—the spice and sweetness, the toast and the cream. But we are also after meaning, and meaning is what you feel when you realize people you will never meet gave you an hour of calm with their labor. There is a sensory map to the ritual. Sight arrives first: the warm color of whiskey, the chalk line of ash stacking like fresh snow, the lazy blue ribbons of smoke. Smell comes next, tugging memories out of storage—campfires, barns, leather, maple, rain on hot pavement, old books. Feel shows up in your fingers and chest: the rounded glass cool in your palm, the soft give of a properly humidified cigar, the heat of smoke that somehow calms more than it excites. Sound is small but present: a cork easing free, a soft clink of glass on wood, the friendly murmur of a lounge at half volume. Taste itself is a moving target. The first quarter inch of a cigar can be bright or peppery; the middle fat and sweet; the final inches dark and honest. Whiskey starts with an entry, broadens across the tongue, then lingers if it has anything worth saying. When you alternate the two, a new conversation happens. The oak from the pour reaches back into the cedar from the humidor. The spice from the rye routes through the retrohale and finds cinnamon in the smoke. A honeyed bourbon softens a bold ligero. A peated dram meets cocoa and espresso like old neighbors leaning over a fence. Some nights you smoke and sip alone because quiet is the only thing that fits. Other nights you sit among people you know or people you just met. A cigar lounge is a strange fountain that turns strangers into neighbors in a single hour. Name tags are optional. Politics get checked at the door not by rule but by instinct; nobody wants to ruin a

good thing. People ask what you are smoking, not what you make a year. The only status symbol that counts is generosity—who brings a bottle to share, who offers a light, who saves the good chair for the late regular. The conversations wander. Work, kids, cars, ballgames, the weather, and the soft ache of missing people who are gone. Someone tells a story that has been told before and somehow it is funnier tonight. A new guy asks a basic question and gets a dozen helpful answers instead of an online pile-on. The old-timer who never hurries shows a rookie how to fix a canoeing burn with patience and a steady flame. There is advice here, but there is also a kind of mercy. No one at a lounge expects you to be anything but a person trying to enjoy an hour. The allure is not just community; it is also permission. You are allowed to be present. You are allowed to be simple. Your phone can sleep without the world ending. You can stare at nothing and think about everything. The cigar does not complain if you are silent. The whiskey is not jealous if you take five minutes between sips. If modern life has a trap, it is the lie that you must earn every breath with output. Whiskey and cigars do not fight that battle for you— they just point to the door and invite you to step through. — A common objection to all this is that it is indulgent. The answer is that it is—but not in the way critics think. It is not decadent like buying a boat you cannot afford. It is not loud like chasing attention. It is indulgent in the older sense: giving yourself leave to enjoy a simple thing deeply and responsibly. Nobody confuses a good steak for gluttony; they call it dinner. Whiskey and cigars, approached with the same respect, are dinner for the parts of you that work hard and need a reason to exhale. Moderation is the quiet backbone of the experience. A single pour, not a parade. A single cigar, not a chain. Plenty of water. Something to eat. You do not white-knuckle the night and call it living. You let the hour be enough and keep tomorrow in mind. Paradoxically, moderation makes the flavors better. You are not blasting your senses; you are tuning them. When you leave the lounge wanting just one more sip or one more inch of ash, you did it right. Pairings are part instinct, part exploration. There are no referees, but there are good starting points. If a bourbon blooms with vanilla and baking spice, try it with a medium-bodied cigar that leans toward nuts and toast; the combination comes out like pecan pie on Thanksgiving. If a rye shouts black pepper and citrus, set it against a cigar with cream and hay to round off its corners. If a Scotch brings peat and sea air, meet it with a cigar that carries cocoa and espresso so the smoke lines up with the shore. Rituals are as individual as fingerprints. Some line the cap with a wet fingertip before cutting and swear the wrapper stays happier. Some toast the foot at an angle and turn the cigar slowly, believing that patience at the start pays off all the way down. Some add a drop of water to whiskey and call it the key that unlocks the room. None of these moves are mandatory, and none are wrong if they make the experience better for you. The only universal rule is respect —respect for the craft that brought the bottle and the box to your hand. Respect extends to the people around you. Smoke is real and it travels; you aim it away from faces. Ash belongs in an ashtray, not on the floor. If someone asks what you are enjoying, you answer like a neighbor, not a gatekeeper. If a new smoker is excited about a budget stick, you remember your first victories and let them be proud. If an old smoker brings something rare and offers a taste, you accept with gratitude and without fuss. The lounge works because people choose to make it work. The blue-collar heart of this culture beats strong. You will see construction workers next to accountants, nurses next to machinists, veterans next to teenagers home from trade school. The pairing does not ask for a résumé. It asks only that you show up ready to relax and treat the moment like it matters. There is a quiet pride in working with your hands and then using those same hands to light a cigar you bought with honest money. There is a quiet pride in pouring a whiskey you chose carefully because you earned the hour it will season. Craft is not only in the making; it is in the choosing. You do not need to chase every limited edition or buy into every hype cycle. Find the distilleries you trust and keep their bottles near. Find the brands whose rollers make cigars that burn straight and taste like the description on the band. Explore, sure, but do not let curiosity turn into stress. The point is not to collect trophies. The point is to collect good hours. If you want to understand why this pairing keeps winning new converts while keeping old loyalists, look at how it meets the basic human needs we pretend we do not have. We need a sense of control over our time. We need a sense

of mastery over something, even if it is just lighting evenly and tasting caramel under the oak. We need company that is not judgmental and silence that is not lonely. We need beauty that can be held in a hand—a shape of a glass, a ribbon of smoke, a simple label with an honest age statement. There are myths that deserve a quick burial. One is that you must be rich to enjoy any of this. Not true. A simple, well-made bourbon can be a revelation beside a cigar that costs less than lunch. Another is that you must be an expert before you are allowed to have an opinion. Also untrue. Your palate is your license. If you taste apple pie, then apple pie is there. If you taste campfire and honey and a hint of orange peel, then that is what you taste. A third myth is that there is one correct way to do any of this. There isn't. There are better ways and worse ways, and most of them can be learned in an evening by paying attention. Let's talk mechanics for a minute, because mechanics are part of pleasure. Cut the cap cleanly. If the draw feels like sucking a milkshake through a coffee stirrer, take a little more off; if it feels like a wind tunnel, slow your cadence and the cigar might still behave. Toast the foot with patience; you are warming, not igniting a rocket. Take the first puffs in short sips, not gulps. Let the smoke touch your palate and leave through your nose if you can, because retrohale is where the hidden music plays. Environment matters. A rainy afternoon under a covered patio produces a different chapter than a bright Saturday with a ballgame on the TV at the lounge. Music changes things. Silence changes things. If you are at home, crack a window or step outside and listen to the neighborhood go by. If you are at the lounge, choose a seat that lets you see the humidor door open and close. Watching other people choose their hour is a small entertainment by itself. The humidor, even if it is just one single walk-in, is a library of possibilities. You learn to read the shelves the way a fisherman reads water. The top might hold stronger blends, the middle the daily drivers, the bottom the delicate ones that prefer shade and patience. You notice the boxes that empty fast—local favorites—and the ones that gather dust —hidden gems waiting for a curious hand. Opening that door is like stepping into warm, fragrant weather. You do not rush. You let your eyes pass over bands and wood grain and the quiet confidence of good tobacco at rest. Whiskey shelves tell stories too. There are the steady companions— the bottles you can count on for a good pour with no drama. There are the seasonal visitors—the high-proof monsters that wake you up in winter and the gentle, floral drams that sing in spring. There are the oddballs you keep for friends who like adventure: something finished in a strange cask, something from a young distillery that made a smart gamble and won. If you do it right, your shelf does not look like a museum. It looks like an invitation. — Occasion is the third partner in the pairing. A new job calls for a pour with enough character to match your pride. A farewell demands a cigar that burns slow and steady while you say what needs saying and leave what needs leaving unsaid. Tuesday after a long day needs nothing fancy—just honest flavor and a chair that fits. The mistake is to wait only for special occasions. The better rule is to make occasions out of ordinary nights when you need a reason to be grateful.

Gratitude is the secret spice in all of this. Gratitude turns a forty-dollar bottle into a feast and a five-dollar cigar into a blessing. Gratitude notices the hands that made the thing, the weather that shaped it, the time that softened it. Gratitude makes you the kind of person who shares the last two inches with a friend because the story is better when it is shared. Gratitude means you say thanks to the staff, tip fair, and leave the place a little better than you found it.

There is a philosophy hiding in the smoke and the sip. It says that life is not a problem to be solved; it is a thing to be experienced. It says that attention is your most valuable possession, and where you aim it shapes your days. It says that comfort is not an enemy of growth; sometimes comfort is the soil where good thoughts finally sprout. It says that tradition is not a cage; it is a handrail on a staircase you are climbing for the first time. You learn about yourself when you pay attention to small pleasures. Maybe you prefer the first third of a cigar because it is hopeful and bright, or maybe you live for the heavy last act where the flavors get dark and honest. Maybe you like your whiskey neat because you trust it, or with a cube because you like to watch it open like a flower. Maybe you smoke faster when you are anxious and need to be reminded to slow down. Maybe you find that you talk more when you pour rye and listen more when you pour bourbon. Noticing these little truths is its own kind of education.

There will be off nights. A cigar will tunnel because you distracted yourself and puffed too hard. A pour will taste thin because your palate is tired from spicy food. You will drop ash on your jeans and discover pinholes two washes later. You will overshoot your bedtime because the conversation got good. None of this is failure. It is practice. The next night you will rotate the cigar more, drink water between drams, and put the ashtray in a smarter place. A craft this forgiving is worth learning. If you need permission to make the ritual yours, here it is. Keep a little notebook or a note on your phone. Jot down the cigar, the bottle, the company, and the mood in the room. Write one sentence about the flavor and three sentences about the night around it. Years from now you will not care that the cigar tasted like walnut and graham cracker; you will care that it was the night your friend told a hard truth and you were there to hear it, or the night your kid called with good news, or the night the rain hit the tin roof just right. Every culture worth keeping has ways to mark time. Some light candles. Some say prayers. Some raise glasses and lift smoke. None of these are accidents. They are the shape we give to gratitude and memory. Whiskey and cigars do not belong to any one nation or tribe. They belong to anyone willing to treat an hour like a gift. That is why the pairing keeps finding new homes far from where it began, and why it feels familiar even the first time you try it. The health we get from these moments is not measured only in charts. There is health in calm, health in friendship, health in honest conversation, and health in having something to look forward to after a long day. This book will talk about the scientific side in other chapters, but it begins here because the science only matters if the experience is worth protecting. You protect what you love. You love what you understand. Understanding starts with paying attention, and attention starts with an hour in a chair with a glass and a good cigar. If you are new to all this, start simple. Ask for help. Tell the shopkeeper what you usually like—sweet, spicy, creamy, bright—and let them steer you toward a bottle and a cigar that fit. Do not worry about looking inexperienced; the only people who sneer are the ones who forgot their first time. Cut, light, sip, and notice. Take your time. Put your phone face down. Breathe. If you do nothing else, do that, and you will already be ahead of most of the world. If you have been around a while, teach without preaching. Remember that nobody came to the lounge to be scolded. Share your wins and your misses. Let the new folks discover their own favorites even if your favorites are different. Offer a pour or a stick when the occasion calls for it, and accept one when it is offered to you. The quiet economy of generosity keeps the room warmer than any heater. When the night ends, end it well. Do not chase a second pour unless the first one taught you to ask for it. Set the nub down before it turns bitter and let the smoke drift into memory. Thank the people you sat with and the people who worked to keep the place clean and the humidor healthy. Step outside and notice the air. Walk to your car a little slower than you arrived. Carry the calm with you as long as you can. And then, on another day that needs it, do it again. Not because you are collecting notches in a hobby belt, but because the hour you spent was worth more than the hour you might have given to noise. Because you built a small tradition in a loud world. Because the glass and the cigar taught you, gently, to be where your feet are. That is the timeless allure of whiskey and cigars. It is not a trick, not a marketing slogan, not a costume for people who want to look important. It is a way of giving shape to gratitude. It is a craft you can learn in one night and spend a lifetime refining. It is a home you can carry with you wherever a good chair sits and a generous pour waits. It is, at the end of a long day, a reminder that the simple things done with care are the ones that last.

CHAPTER 2

A Deep Breath of History

History is something you can hold in your hands. A cigar between the fingers, a glass of whiskey in the other — both are artifacts of people and places, of seasons and skills that stretch backward farther than a quick glance suggests. Before they were luxuries, they were solutions. Before they became symbols, they were simply the best ideas people had for preserving what the earth gave them. The story of whiskey and cigars is the story of weather and wood, of migration and markets, of faithfulness to craft across lifetimes.

Take a slow breath and imagine leaf and grain at the beginning. Tobacco is a plant that likes sun and patience. Grain is a grass that likes rain and soil that holds it. One becomes smoke, the other becomes spirit, but neither path is inevitable. People had to notice, to fail, to try again, and to pass along what worked. That is the part too many histories miss: the countless hands who quietly learned how to turn a season into a story you could taste. LEAF

BEFORE EMPIRE Tobacco was sacred long before it was fashionable. On this continent, different nations treated the leaf as a gift meant for ceremony, medicine, and treaty. Pipes were carved with care; smoke meant words were serious. European sailors met the plant and brought it home as a curiosity. Curiosity became habit. Habit became commerce. The Spanish crown claimed early control of the trade and built its factories where the best leaf grew thick and honest. The word "cigar" likely drifted from "sikar," a Mayan word for smoking, and followed ships and ledgers across the Atlantic. Cuba's western farmlands — Vuelta Abajo — proved to be a miracle of soil and wind for tobacco. Dark, mineralrich dirt and steady breezes made wrappers that gleamed and fillers that sang. Not far away, the Dominican Republic, Nicaragua, and Honduras had their own gifts of sun and rain. In Seville, factories gathered knowledge; rollers learned to make a straight burn line and a draw that felt like an invitation. Boxes of Spanish cedar kept humidity and pests at bay and taught the leaf to rest. Over time, the ritual traveled with the box: cedar, paper, band, hand. By the nineteenth century the cigar was both a status symbol and a daily comfort. Immigrants carried the craft into new cities. In the United States, Connecticut farmers learned to raise delicate wrapper under shade, stretching cloth across fields to soften the sun and coax a thin, silky leaf. Tampa became a cigar town, and Ybor City spoke Spanish in the morning and commerce all day. The lector read newspapers and novels aloud to the rollers as their hands moved every minute they were awake. The work was hard, the pride quiet, and the aroma in those rooms could make a stranger hungry for a smoke. The twentieth century brought shock and reshaping. After the Cuban Revolution and embargo, some of the leaf and much of the know-how scattered to new homes. Families who had perfected blends in Havana started over in Santiago, Estelí, and Danlí. Seed crossed borders in envelopes. Fields were tested by hand and by hope. Terroir — that complicated marriage of place and practice — wrote new chapters without erasing the old ones. Even today, when someone describes a cigar as "Cuban-style," they are talking about a memory of balance and combustion as much as origin. GRAIN BEFORE GLAMOUR Whiskey started as a solution too: how to keep grain from spoiling and how to transport value without hauling a wagon full of sacks down muddy roads. In the old world, monks and farmers learned how to turn barley into beer and then into uisce beatha — water of life. Ireland and Scotland wrote early chapters in different dialects. Pot stills bubbled. Barley malted on floors where men raked it with wooden tools. Spirits came off the still harsh and bright and then turned patient inside wood. Tax collectors and laws shaped whiskey almost as much as geology. In Scotland, the exciseman chased illicit distillers through heather and hill, and the glens filled with secrets that later became stories.

The 1830s brought Aeneas Coffey's continuous still to Britain, an invention that allowed lighter grain spirit in volume. Blending took center stage: sturdy, flavorful pot-still malt married to gentle, consistent grain whisky. Names that now seem eternal were once risky experiments carried by merchants with good palates and steady hands. Across the Atlantic, grain met different weather and different needs. Rye loved the mid-Atlantic. Corn loved the limestone soils and iron-free water of Kentucky. Frontier life rewarded practicality: a barrel of whiskey kept better than a wagonload of corn, and it could be traded, taxed, or tithed. Early American whiskey was rough by modern standards, but the genius was there — charcoal and charred oak turned raw heat into color and flavor. By the 1790s the federal government learned that taxing whiskey was a way to measure and manage a young nation's commerce; the Whiskey Rebellion wrote a loud footnote to that lesson. As the country matured, so did its distillers. Recipes became more deliberate. The trade learned to trust fresh char on new oak. Kentucky made a name for bourbon; Pennsylvania and Maryland kept faith with rye. Quality laws followed. Bottled-in-Bond asked distillers to put their name and reputation on the line and to age spirit under supervision so buyers knew what they were getting. Later acts hammered out fair labeling. By then the barrel had become a time machine. What went in clear came out with stories. THE LONG WINTER AND THE THAW The twentieth century gave and took in equal measure. Prohibition tried to turn off the stills and the cigar cutters alike. It did not kill either craft, but it did bend them. Whiskey went medicinal on paper and entrepreneurial in the shadows. Cigars moved to back rooms and quiet parlors. When the lights came back on, tastes had shifted. Lighter beers came into fashion. Cocktails returned with color and umbrellas. The postwar decades saw bourbon nap while Scotch taught the world to ask for blends by name.

Cigars rode their own waves. They were everywhere in black-and-white photos and then disappeared from some rooms as the tide of warnings and new rules rose. Yet the premium cigar — a handmade thing meant for an hour, not a habit — kept its dignity. Families rebuilt in new countries. Fields learned new seasons. A generation discovered that good tobacco had many homes and that a straight burn line owed more to care than to nationality. By the late twentieth and early twenty-first century, both crafts woke up strong. The bourbon renaissance reminded America of its own inheritance. Small distilleries sprouted like new growth in a forest that had been logged too hard. Some were clumsy at first; most got better fast. Barrels were finished in wine casks, port pipes, sherry butts; rye shook off its dusty reputation and started telling citrus-and-pepper stories again. Meanwhile, cigar makers blended with a painter's eye — pulling spice from Estelí, earth from Jalapa, cream from Santiago — and matched combustion to flavor so the experience traveled in a straight line from foot to band. BOXES, BARRELS, AND THE PATIENCE IN WOOD Open a humidor and you open a museum of wood and time. Spanish cedar does more than smell good; it moderates humidity and repels the bugs that love leaf as much as you do. Boxes breathe slowly; walk-in humidors breathe a little faster. Either way, the wood becomes a character in the story. A cigar resting in good cedar picks up a calm that shows up later as a cool burn and a clean finish. Ask anyone who has smoked a stick too soon: time is the ingredient you cannot fake. The barrel says the same thing in a different accent. New American oak — its pores opened by fire — offers vanilla and caramel, toast and spice. European oak leans toward dried fruit and nuts. The former wine or sherry that once sat in a cask leaves whispers behind, and whiskey learns to speak with a broader vocabulary. Inside the barrel, temperature and season push spirit into and out of the oak. Summers write fast; winters write small. Over years, the raw edges sand down. A good distiller knows when to wait and when to stop waiting. PEOPLE IN THE STORY Histories like to chase kings and characters, but the heart of this story is working people. There are famous names, sure — the statesman who lit after victories and defeats, the novelist whose desk ashtray never cooled — but the truth lives with farmers who plant and top and harvest, the fermenters who watch the temperature of a pilón like it is their own pulse, the roller who feels with a fingertip whether the draw will be easy and true. The cooper who hears a stave ring right. The warehouse hand who learns the smell of a leaker without seeing the stain. The modern lounge manager who keeps the single humidor healthy and the regular's chair clean belongs in this history, too. So does the shop owner who teaches a newcomer how to cut without tearing a cap. So does the bartender who pours light and calls you by name. Crafts survive when communities protect them. No law ever preserved a good tradition without people choosing to love it on Tuesday nights after work. TRADE WINDS AND CROSSINGS The pairing of whiskey and cigars did not have to happen, but history kept setting the table. Ships that carried casks carried leaf. Port towns tasted both. Merchants who had money to lend and time to spend brought cigars and spirits into the same rooms and discovered that the flavors knew how to dance together. Oak, toast, and spice in the glass met cedar, cream, and cocoa in the smoke, and the handshake felt natural. Even the tools overlapped: wood, fire, air, and time. Barrels that once held fortified wine were recycled because they were strong and available; whiskey learned to love

what sherry and port had left behind. Cedar boxes once chosen for practical virtues turned into icons. When you see a ribbon around a cask or a band on a cigar, you are seeing fashion that grew out of function. History is full of accidents that, once they happen, look like destiny.

DECLINE, PANIC, AND THE RETURN TO BETTER

Every craft faces a season when it forgets itself. Whiskey chased novelty until some shelves looked like a costume party. Cigars ballooned in size and strength until the first third felt like a dare. Markets reward big and loud for a while and then wander back toward balance. What brought both worlds home was the same thing that made them worth having in the first place: flavor that tells the truth and an experience that respects your time. Good makers did not argue with trends; they just kept making things that tasted like honesty. LAWS, LABELS, AND THE LANGUAGE OF TRUST Regulations shape history as surely as revolutions do. There are labels that mean something because people before you fought to give them meaning. "Straight" whiskey, "bottled-in-bond," and geographic statements about where leaf grew — these are forms of trust. They tell you what a bottle or a box must be to earn the words on its face. Are they perfect? No. But they push in the direction of honesty, and honesty is a worker's virtue. If the band says one country and the flavors say another, your palate is allowed to vote. THE HISTORY YOU CAN TASTE You can taste the old world in a dram that smells like barley drying over a fire. You can taste Caribbean sun in a wrapper that shines with natural oils. You can taste midwestern summers and white-oak forests in a bourbon that wears caramel like a warm coat. History is not abstract when it touches your tongue. To pay attention to those tastes is to respect the people behind them. If you call out walnut and hay in a cigar or orange peel and clove in a whiskey, you are reading history out loud. Pairing by history is its own kind of fun. If you pour a Scotch finished in sherry casks, try it with a cigar that leans cocoa and dried fruit, and let the old trade routes do the work for you. If you reach for a rye born near cold rivers, pair it with a creamy, nut-forward cigar from a valley that likes morning fog; watch the pepper meet the cream like two neighbors leaning across a fence. If you pour a bourbon that speaks in vanilla and cornbread, find a cigar with toast and honey and let the porch swing set the rhythm. WHY THIS CHAPTER MATTERS A book about health has to honor the reasons a thing is worth keeping. If cigars and whiskey were just vices, the story would be short. But the truth is longer. These are crafts that turned raw materials into meaning. They shaped towns and paid mortgages. They taught patience. They made rooms where a stranger could sit and leave a friend. When critics aim at the cartoon version of either, history is the antidote. History puts names and families and fields and seasons back into the picture so we remember what we are talking about. This chapter is not a defense. It is an introduction. If you carry these scenes into the rest of the book — the barns and stills, the barrels and boxes — you will see the science in context later. You will understand why moderation is the right word and why ritual has real effects on the heart and mind.

You will understand why some of us get a little misty-eyed talking about a walk-in humidor that smells like cedar and possibility, or a rackhouse where dust motes float in a sunbeam and every barrel looks like a promise. THE STORY CONTINUES History does not end; it accumulates. New seed crosses oceans. New barrels are charred in new patterns. A blender tries a combination that shouldn't work and it does. A distiller waits one more summer and catches lightning in a bottle for a few hundred people lucky enough to be in the right shop on the right day. Someone's first cigar happens on a night that changes the shape of their week. Someone's first good whiskey teaches them that flavor isn't a list of notes; it's a memory that decides to stay. If you listen closely, you can hear history breathing in the background of the lounge — air moving in the humidor, ice sighing in the glass, boots on the floor, and that low, satisfied "mm-hmm" when a sip and a puff meet in the middle. The work of generations is present tense in moments like that. It is not nostalgia. It is gratitude with a flavor.

So take a deep breath of history when you light and when you pour. You are not escaping the world; you are entering it more honestly — aware of the hands and years that brought this hour to you. Tomorrow's chapter will talk about what the research says happens in bodies and brains when we practice ritual, pace, and friendship. But none of that would matter if the hour weren't beautiful. And it is. It has been for a very long time. PORTS, WORKSHOPS, AND THE GEOGRAPHY OF TASTE Follow the map and you can follow the flavors. New Orleans tasted early American whiskey alongside Caribbean rum and learned to serve both with confidence; Liverpool and Glasgow put their hands on casks that crossed the Atlantic and came home with stories in oak; Seville and Cádiz smelled like leaf and salt at once. Port cities were the places where barrels rolled and boxes breathed, where the vocabulary of pairing was born informally in taverns and counting houses. Even today, when a lounge sits a thousand miles from salt water, you can trace its habits back to a harbor city where sailors, shopkeepers, and bankers compared notes after work and discovered that oak and cedar like each other. Shade-grown Connecticut wrapper deserves its own footnote in history's ledger. Stretching cheesecloth over fields to soften the sun was both a practical trick and a statement of intent: we will take the time to make a delicate thing. That leaf wrapped blends from Havana in the old days and wraps blends from Santiago and Estelí now, tying centuries together with a pale, silky ribbon. Ybor City's lectores carried a different ribbon — sound — tying workers to the world outside by reading news and novels while hands moved leaf to leaf. In those factories, flavor and story grew up together. The diaspora of Cuban families after the embargo is a chapter written in courage and stubborn hope. They took seed that had names like heirlooms and planted it in soils that did not yet know them — Jalapa's red earth, the rich beds near Danlí, the gentle slopes outside Santiago. They rebuilt fermentation barns and convinced new stacks of cedar to remember the old songs. Decades later, their children blend from memory and from curiosity at the same time, which is how traditions stay honest. REGULATIONS, REMEDIES, AND THE STRANGE GIFTS OF LAW The American Whiskey Rebellion is more than a trivia answer; it is proof that alcohol was already a language of value on the frontier. People do not fight taxes on things that do not matter. The later Bottled-in-Bond Act did something quietly radical: it gave regular buyers a way to trust a label without knowing a distiller personally. In a young nation full of hustlers and honest men alike, that mattered. During Prohibition, when whiskey survived as "medicine," doctors wrote prescriptions that looked a lot like common sense wearing a tie. Premium cigars, never made for compulsion, found quieter rooms during that same era. Humidors lived behind paneled doors and on covered porches, and the etiquette of offering someone a light became even more important because it was an invitation to talk where talk was safe. When the long winter ended, both whiskey and cigars returned to the daylight with new scars and new stories — and maybe with a deeper understanding that their survival depended on respect more than rebellion. WOOD, FIRE, WATER, AIR — AND TIME Barrels and boxes teach the same lessons in different dialects. Char levels are a simple way to talk about fire's work — lighter char for gentler sweetness, deeper alligator char for heavier caramel and smoke — but wood does not follow charts as if they were law. Each tree is its own biography. Warehouse placement matters: top floors run hot and write fast; bottom floors run cool and write small. On the cigar side, a single walk-in humidor breathes with the seasons like a friendly animal. Keep it near sixty-five to seventy percent humidity and in the low seventies for temperature, and the leaf will repay you with calm combustion and clean flavor. Treat the wood with respect and it becomes a patient partner; ignore it and it will teach you humility. PEOPLE, AGAIN We should keep the spotlight where it belongs: on workers. A pilón tender in Estelí knows by the feel of his palm whether the ferment runs too hot. A cooper in Kentucky hears a stave ring and knows which hoop needs love. A blender in Santiago drops a percentage point from one ligero and adds a pinch of seco and smiles because combustion and flavor finally shook hands. A bartender in a small Midwestern shop remembers you like a short

pour neat and saves the outside chair because he knows you like to watch the rain. Craft lives or dies on these small acts of care. PAIRING HISTORY WITH THE PRESENT History is not just what happened. It is what keeps happening. When you pour a rye with orange-peel confidence and set it next to a creamy, nut-forward cigar, you are reenacting a trade between cold rivers and warm valleys. When you pair a sherry-finished Scotch with a cocoa-leaning cigar, you are letting Iberian cooperage whisper to Caribbean soil. When you reach for a high-corn bourbon that smells like cornbread and vanilla and you meet it with toast and honey in the smoke, you can almost hear a porch swing set the rhythm. A LAST LOOK BACK BEFORE WE GO FORWARD If this chapter seems generous with gratitude, it is because gratitude is faithful to the facts. People made these crafts with patience and stubbornness, and those qualities are good for human beings. A world that forgets how to wait forgets how to feel. Whiskey and cigars have always been about teaching waiting to be a friend instead of a punishment. If you keep that in mind, the science we will talk about next will land in the right place — not as permission to overdo anything, but as encouragement to keep a ritual that shapes better hours. So take one more deep breath of history. Smell cedar and oak and the clean promise of barley and leaf. Think about ships and trains and trucks and hands. Think about evenings when a worker washed up and sat down and decided that an hour should be shaped like gratitude. Then turn the page. The next part of our conversation belongs to what researchers have learned about ritual and attention and the chemistry of calm — and how a good chair, a good glass, and a good cigar can help you find it.

CHAPTER 3

Science, Smoke, and Spirits

This chapter isn't a lecture; it's a flashlight. We're going to shine it on what actually happens in your body and mind when you sit down with a glass and a cigar and give the hour your attention. No miracle claims, no scare tactics, just what's reasonable to understand and what's worth doing on purpose. The short version is that ritual, pace, and company change the way your nervous system runs the show. The long version is better, because it lets you use that knowledge to make the hour healthier and more satisfying. WHAT THE BODY DOES WHEN YOU SLOW DOWN Your body has two main settings for daily life: ready-to-run and ready-to-recover. People use fancier words— sympathetic and parasympathetic—but the idea is simple. Ready-to-run is the ramped-up state that gets you to the jobsite, keeps you alert in traffic, and helps you move when the weather turns. Ready-to-recover is the downshift that handles repair, digestion, and the feeling that your shoulders finally dropped out of your ears. A lot of modern life keeps the dial stuck on ready-to-run. A well-made hour with a cigar and a small pour is a manual override back toward recovery. Part of that override is breath. Lighting a cigar the right way makes you breathe slow and controlled. You draw gently. You pause. You exhale. You do it again a minute later. That rhythm is not an accident; it's a lever. Slow, regular breathing tells the body to ease off the gas and put a little more work into the brakes. Your heart listens. Your stomach listens. The knot between your shoulder blades listens. Even people who don't use fancy gadgets can feel this when they stop rushing and start noticing that the smoke moves like a tide instead of a siren. Another part is posture. The hour starts when you sit down like you mean it. A heavy chair and a glass with a little weight to it make the body feel anchored. You're not bracing yourself to sprint; you're letting yourself settle. Muscles that have been quiet-tense all day get permission to loosen. Your jaw unclenches. Your brow smooths out.

These are not just niceties. They're signals. The tight jaw tells the brain there's trouble; the relaxed one says "We're safe." Your own face is a microphone. Then there's pace. A cigar teaches it without speeches. Puff too fast and the cigar punishes you with heat and bitterness. Sip too fast and the whiskey goes loud and shallow. When you learn the pace of each, you're learning the

pace of yourself. A lot of stress is a problem of rhythm—too much noise in the same window of time. When you space the puffs and sips, you're carving room for your nervous system to catch up and settle down. That's not theory; that's practice you can feel in your chest. THE LIMPET THAT LIVES IN YOUR NOSE People joke that smell is the most honest sense. There's science hiding in the joke. The nose has a VIP lane to the parts of the brain that handle memory and feeling. That's why a single whiff —barn wood, rain on hot pavement, orange peel catching flame—can move you faster than a long conversation. A cigar and a dram are smell-forward on purpose. The glass tips and the nose gets there before the tongue does. The foot of the cigar warms and a little cloud lifts before the first real puff. Smell walks ahead and opens doors. Why does that matter? Because moods are easier to steer through the senses than through speeches. You can tell yourself to calm down and your body shrugs. You can smell vanilla and oak and your body says "We've been here before, and it's fine." You can smell cedar and bread and a hint of cocoa and your shoulders drop one notch. The scents aren't magic; they ride old roads your brain already trusts. If you've had a good hour in a good chair with good people a hundred times, your nose can find that street in a hurry on the hundred and first. TASTE, TOUCH, AND THE REWARD OF ATTENTION Taste gets all the headlines, but touch carries half the story. The weight of the glass. The curve under your fingers. The soft spring of a properly humidified cigar. These little signals tell your nervous system that you're handling something real and steady. If your day was screens and noise and changing demands, a solid object that behaves itself is a small rescue. Taste is a movie, not a snapshot. Whiskey walks in, talks mid-sentence, and lingers on the porch. The start, the middle, the finish. A cigar does the same in slow motion: bright or peppery at the foot, mellow in the middle, honest and darker near the band. Paying attention to that arc is a kind of training. You're practicing noticing. You're practicing patience. The brain likes tasks with a reward at the end, and holding a thread of flavor across a minute or two is a human-sized challenge with a human-sized payoff. THE SOCIAL SCIENCE YOU CAN FEEL You don't need a study to tell you that good company is good for you, but it helps to know what you're tapping into. People are herd creatures with front doors and car keys. We do better when we belong. A cigar lounge makes belonging easy without making it complicated. You have a shared language—

labels, cuts, wrappers, proofs, pours— and you have a shared goal—an honest hour. That gets you most of the way to feeling like you fit, even if you met five minutes ago. Belonging calms. The body keeps an eye out for threat. When the room feels safe, that watcher can take a break. You don't have to scan for danger. You don't have to defend your corner. You can ask what someone else is smoking and care what they say. That calm is not just warm feelings. It's lower muscle tone and easier breath and less of that background hum that wears you out by dinner. Call it community. Call it fellowship. Call it Tuesday. Whatever the name, your body recognizes it. RISK, REALITY, AND HOW TO AIM THE HOUR Let's talk straight. Cigars are smoke. Whiskey is alcohol. Neither one is broccoli. They come with risk that you can't spin away with poetry. But risk isn't a switch—off or on. It's a set of dials you can set in smarter or dumber directions. "How much, how often, how fast, and what else is going on?" Those questions draw the map. How much: The simplest pattern I know is one cigar for the hour and one modest pour that you stretch. Add water if you want the nose to open or the proof to relax. If you're thirsty, drink actual water. Your body knows the difference and thanks you for it. How often: Ritual means it's not constant. A couple nights a week is a very different animal from every night, and every night is a different animal from all day. If you make the hour special by keeping it scarce, you get more joy for less cost. That's not discipline for its own sake. It's just good arithmetic.

How fast: Slow is your friend. Fast is a liar. The same amount rushed feels like more and lands like worse. If you linger and listen, the flavors bloom and the body has time to keep up. If you race, you make yourself a job out of something that wasn't supposed to be work. What else is going on: Food matters. Sleep matters. Medicine matters. If you're on something that doesn't play well with alcohol, you skip the drink and keep the cigar—or skip both and keep the fellowship. If you're short on sleep, you choose an earlier hour or a milder cigar and you put the phone down sooner. Grown people make grown choices. That's half the pleasure. THE DIFFERENCE BETWEEN A RITUAL AND A HABIT Rituals are built; habits happen. A ritual is a shape you give to time because you've decided it deserves a shape. A habit is a rut you fall into without thinking. The same cigar and the same glass can sit at the center of either. The difference is attention. When you choose the chair, clean the glass, cut carefully, toast patiently, sip with respect— that's ritual. When you reach for the lighter because you always do and you scroll your phone and the ash grows crooked while your mind is somewhere else—that's habit. Ritual trains attention, and attention trains the rest of you. People pay for apps to help them be mindful. You already have a built-in practice if you want it. Cut the cap, toast the foot, sip, breathe, taste, notice, talk. You can do all of that without turning your life into a self-improvement project. The fancy word "mindfulness" just means "be here for your own evening."

— HOW THE LOUNGE MAKES YOU HEALTHIER (WITHOUT TALKING ABOUT HEALTH) A good lounge is a gym for the parts of you that don't wear sneakers. You practice patience when someone takes a little longer to tell a story but you let them finish. You practice generosity when you pour a finger for a friend or offer a light to a stranger. You practice respect when you keep your smoke aimed where it won't bother anyone and you clean up your ash. None of that shows up on a blood test, but it shows up in how your day goes. You also practice boundaries without speeches. A lounge is both public and private. You can be friendly without having to perform. You can listen without having to fix. You can complain about your team and be forgiven because everyone else has a team to complain about too. When you walk out the door, you feel lighter for reasons that have nothing to do with nicotine or ethanol. You feel lighter because your nervous system got an hour off from being in charge of everything.

SENSORY TRAINING: WHY PAIRING IS A CLASSROOM Nobody walks into a lounge knowing how to taste. You learn the same way you learned to swing a hammer or fry an egg: you do it and pay attention to what happens. Pairing helps because it gives the senses a partner. Vanilla in the whiskey wakes up toast in the cigar. Pepper in the cigar makes orange in the whiskey speak up. Cocoa in the smoke calms the loud parts of a high-proof pour. If you play it like a game—match the nose, match the mid, match the finish—you train your brain to hold more than one thing at once without rushing. That's useful far outside the lounge. You also learn your own map. Some people live for the bright start of a cigar, when everything is clean and eager. Others love the middle, where the flavors stack like a good sandwich. Some wait for the last inches, where the honesty shows and the soft notes turn dark. The whiskey tells its own story in parallel. Maybe you like rye because it keeps your attention. Maybe you like bourbon because it warms without arguing. Maybe you like Scotch because it smells like old wood and wind. There's no right answer. There's only your answer and your willingness to notice it change over time. THE HOUR AND THE CLOCK Stress is often an argument with time. There's never enough, or it's the wrong kind, or it's in the wrong place. One of the smartest things you can do with whiskey and cigars is use them to set a firm start and a firm stop. The cigar is an hourglass with ash instead of sand. When it's over, the hour is over. That helps your brain. You don't pretend the evening will last forever and then feel guilty when it doesn't. You know the shape of what you promised yourself

and you keep it. The clock helps with moderation too. You can't hurry a good cigar much without ruining it. You can't hurry a good pour much without missing it. If you keep to the natural speed of each, you're already protecting yourself from your own bad ideas. People get into trouble with alcohol when they chase a feeling instead of a flavor. If you keep chasing flavor, you stay on safer ground. SLEEP, TIMING, AND HOW TO NOT SABOTAGE TOMORROW You can make the night beautiful and still respect the morning. Nicotine is a push. Alcohol is a lull that sometimes springs back. Put those together too late and you pay for it in bed. The fix is simple: start earlier, choose gentler, and give yourself water and time. If you put the cigar out before it turns bitter and you put the glass down before you stop tasting it, you've already made tomorrow easier. Another fix: leave a buffer. Give yourself thirty minutes after the last puff and last sip before you chase the pillow. Wash your hands. Brush your teeth. Read a page. Stack the ashtray. You're letting your body know the show is over and the crew is striking the set. Your brain likes that kind of signal more than we give it credit for. HYDRATION, FOOD, AND THE QUIET DETAILS THAT CHANGE EVERYTHING A pitcher of water on the table is the cheapest upgrade in the world. You smell more, you taste more, and you wake up happier. Food matters too. A little salt and a little fat keep the whiskey friendly and keep the cigar from feeling like a workout. This isn't about "soaking it up" like some bar myth. It's about giving your body honest fuel so you're not running the ritual on fumes. Pacing your water works the same way as pacing your smoke and your sip. You don't have to make it a chore. Take a sip of water every time the conversation takes a turn. Your palate resets. Your head stays clear. You notice that you're not tempted to pour more than you meant to. That's the science you can taste.

WHO SHOULDN'T PLAY THIS GAME TONIGHT Adults decide for themselves, but honesty helps. If you're driving, you treat the pour like a nose and a taste, not a drink. If you're on medicine that fights with alcohol, you skip it. If you're exhausted, you pick a milder cigar and an earlier hour. If your doctor said no alcohol for reasons that matter, then no alcohol. Nothing about this ritual needs the glass to be beautiful. Ginger ale and ice can be just as pretty in the right light, and your cigar won't complain. And of course some nights you skip the smoke too. Cold, flu, anything that puts your lungs on the defensive—give the leaf a night off. If you're training for something or you need your sleep more than you need your stories, you make the grown choice. This is recreation, not obligation. —

THE EXPECTATION EFFECT (AND HOW TO USE IT WITHOUT LYING TO YOURSELF) The brain is powerful and suggestible. If you walk into the lounge expecting a good hour, you make it easier for the hour to be good. That's not magic; that's attention budgeting. If you expect to rush, you'll rush. If you expect to taste, you'll slow down. If you expect to talk about something real, you'll ask a better question. You can use that on purpose.

Set a tiny intention at the start: "Tonight I'm going to notice the middle of the cigar." Or: "Tonight I'm going to ask that guy about his shop build." The hour will find its shape around small plans like that. There's a flip side—don't talk yourself into disappointment by demanding perfection. Not every bottle opens up. Not every stick draws like a dream. The point isn't to assemble a museum of flawless experiences. The point is to enjoy an honest one and learn how to make more nights land in the sweet spot. Bumps in the road are still part of the road. WHAT WOOD AND LEAF TEACH YOUR BRAIN A barrel is a teacher. An oak tree turns sunlight into lignin and cellulose and all the quiet compounds that taste like vanilla and toast and nuts when fire and time translate them. When you nose a whiskey and call out caramel or

spice, you're not just sniffing labels—you're reading the tree back to itself. The same with a cigar. A wrapper grown under cloth in Connecticut or in the full sun of Estelí tells the story of light and water and patience. Your senses learn to pick up those stories. That learning sticks. People think training the palate is fancy. It isn't. It's repetition, curiosity, and names. When you give a flavor a name —"hay," "cocoa," "orange peel," "cedar"—you make it easier to find again. You wire a little path in your head. Over time those paths make the hour richer. They also make you better at noticing outside the lounge: you catch the smell of rain earlier, you taste the difference in bread baked hot versus warm, you spot when a friend is quieter than usual. Attention in one room trains attention in all the rooms. YOUR OWN MEASUREMENTS (WITHOUT BECOMING A LAB) You don't need a spreadsheet to enjoy yourself. But a little tracking makes you honest to yourself and teaches you what works. Keep a pocket notebook or a note on your phone. Write the cigar, the bottle, the time, the company, and three short lines: one about flavor, one about mood before, one about mood after.

You will see patterns. Maybe high-proof pours make you talkative. Maybe creamy cigars put you in a listening mood. Maybe you sleep better if you keep the hour before nine. That's not the kind of science that argues on TV. That's the kind that makes tomorrow better than today. If you like gadgets, you can go further without being weird about it. Pay attention to your steps or your sleep or your resting heart rate across weeks, not nights. If the ritual helps you feel calmer and keeps you kinder, you'll see it show up in the averages even if any given Tuesday is just a Tuesday. Don't chase numbers. Let numbers confirm what your gut already knows. COURTESY IS A HEALTH PRACTICE The way you behave in a lounge changes the health of everyone else in the room. Aim your smoke. Ask before you move a chair. Keep the humidor door from hanging open. Offer a light. Share a pour when it makes sense. That list looks like manners but feels like medicine. People relax faster around people who are paying attention to others. That's a gift you can give for free. The staff matter too. Tip like you plan to come back. Thank the person who keeps the glasses clean and the ashtrays emptied and the one walk-in humidor happy. Their invisible work turns your ritual into a smooth runway. If you've ever smoked a too-dry cigar or sipped from a lipstick-stained glass, you know how much the quiet details matter. THE MODERATION TOOLBOX Here's a simple toolbox that has never failed me: • Water in reach. Drink it often. • Food before or during—something salty and something with a little fat. • One cigar only. Let it be enough. • One pour you stretch, or two smaller ones spread way out. • A firm stop time and a short wind-down routine. • Nights off—put them on the calendar. • A friend who knows your plan and will nudge you if you drift. • An exit —when the cigar turns bitter or the conversation turns mean, call it. None of that makes the hour less fun. It makes it more fun because you're in charge of it. You don't have to wake up angry at yourself or swear off everything until Friday. You can just live like an adult who knows how to enjoy something without letting it run the table. — WHY THIS IS A HEALTH CHAPTER IN A JOY BOOK If this chapter feels practical, that's on purpose. You can't protect what you love unless you understand it. The surprise is that understanding makes the pleasure bigger, not smaller. Knowing that slow breath helps you downshift doesn't steal the romance from the draw; it adds a layer you can appreciate. Knowing that smell is the fast lane to

old good feelings doesn't make you cynical about why a certain bourbon makes you smile; it makes you grateful to be built the way you are. There will always be people who want to argue in slogans—either everything you enjoy is killing you or everything the critics say is bunk. The truth is simpler and stronger. Enjoyment with attention is good for human beings. Responsibility isn't the enemy of pleasure; it's how pleasure lasts. The hour is a gift when you treat it like one. It's trouble when you treat it like a hiding place. You get to choose. That's the most grown-up sentence in this whole book. A BLUE-COLLAR CHECKLIST (NO WHITE COATS REQUIRED) Before you light: Did you eat? Do you have water? Are you driving later? What time do you want to be done? While you're in it: Are you tasting or chasing? Are you listening as much as you talk? Are you keeping your smoke polite? After: Did you leave the place better than you found it? Did you sleep well? Do you feel grateful? If you can answer those with some pride most nights, you're doing it right. You don't need a diploma. You need a chair, a glass, a good cigar, and a little self-respect. THE PART WHERE WE LOOK AHEAD The next chapters will talk about specific benefits people notice most—heart, head, community—and about myths that need to be retired. We'll leave the lab coats in the lab and carry only what helps in the chair. The theme won't change: ritual, pace, and company turn two old crafts into something that helps a person live better, not worse, when the person treats them like tools instead of toys. For now, give yourself permission to be proud of the hour you know how to build. It's not a loophole. It's not a dodge. It's a small, honest practice that makes the rest of the week easier to carry. You learned the skill the same way you learned every other good thing you know—by paying attention, by listening to people who were better at it, by trying, by failing, and by trying again. So pour carefully. Cut clean. Toast slow. Breathe. Taste. Talk. Laugh. Let the chair hold you up for a while. Leave when the story has a good ending instead of waiting for a bad one. Walk to the door, put your hand on the glass, and feel the night air on your face with a little more gratitude than you had an hour ago. You did something simple and you did it well. That matters. Tomorrow and the next day will carry their share of noise. That's fine. You have a quiet place you can build when you need it. Science can explain pieces of why it works. Craft and history can explain the rest. You don't have to solve the whole mystery to enjoy the light it throws on your life. And when you're ready again, come back to the chair. Bring your best self and your best manners. The bottle and the box will be waiting, and so will the people who know how to make an hour count.

CHAPTER 4

The Heart and the Hearth: Cardiovascular Benefits

A good lounge is a kind of hearth, and the heart likes a hearth. Not a blaze that scorches, not a pile of glowing brag, but a steady, honest fire. The heart is a worker that never clocks out, and it has two main questions for you: Will you give me calm work, and will you give me good rhythms? The rituals around a cigar and a small pour can answer both questions in the right light. This is not a miracle chapter. It's a practical one. We will talk about stress and pace and breath and timing, about posture and warmth and company, and about how to use what you already love to make your heart's job easier instead of harder. Start with the obvious: the heart is a pump, the blood are the deliveries, and the vessels are the roads. But it's also rhythm, and rhythm is the hidden part most of us feel but don't name. A noisy day knocks your rhythm around. A quiet hour can tune it. The pairing of whiskey and cigars, when handled like a craft instead of a contest, gives you tools to tune with. Tools, not excuses. Tools, not slogans. The hearth is there to warm you, not to set the curtains on

fire. WHAT THE HEART WANTS Your heart likes patterns it can trust: steady breath, steady movement, steady rest. It likes the parasympathetic downshift, the "we're safe" signal that ripples out through breath and posture and pace. It likes muscles that are not clenched for no reason. It likes laughter. It likes the kind of companionship where your guard drops without you having to think about it. If you want a short list of things the heart dislikes, it's just the opposites: rush, panic, tightness, loneliness, and the habit of turning every evening into an emergency. A cigar and a small pour will not teach you how to run a marathon, and this chapter isn't pretending they will. But the hour you build around them can do something basic and valuable: it can turn down the noise that keeps your heart idling high for no reason. That matters. Think of it like this: your heart has only so many beats to work with. When you spend too many on worry and whiplash, you're paying a tax you don't need to pay. When you spend an hour teaching your breath to be a metronome and your mind to be present, you're not saving beats in a jar, but you are spending them better. BREATH: THE CHEAPEST TOOL YOU OWN Light a cigar properly and you're halfway to a better heart hour before the first real puff. You're breathing on purpose. You draw gently. You pause. You exhale. You watch the foot glow and settle. That rhythm is more than ceremony. Slow inhale through the nose. Gentle puff at the foot. Full exhale through the mouth. Repeat with space in between. If you do nothing else, do that. Count if you need to: in for four, out for six. You don't need an app; your smoke is the clock. You will feel it in your chest and jaw right away. Shoulders soften. Jaw unlocks. The low muscles near your ribs wake up and do their share. Your heart hears the message. The fancy term is increased vagal tone. The plain language is better brakes. It isn't complicated: slow air in, slower air out, and time between. The cigar helps because it makes you care about the pace. Puff too fast and you get a hot, bitter lesson. Puff right and the flavor keeps its manners. Either way the breath is the teacher behind the lesson.

PACE: RHYTHM YOU CAN SEE The ash is a story you can read with your eyes. If it stacks clean and light, you're pacing well. If it canoes and tunnels, you're rushing or ignoring. This sounds like cigar talk, and it is, but it's also heart talk. A fast, jagged hour pulls the whole system forward like a dog on a leash. A well-paced hour lets the leash go slack. Your heart hates sprinting in place. Let the cigar teach you not to. The pour has its own rhythm. Whiskey is not for gulping and it will punish you if you try. One slow nose, one small sip, one beat of silence while you notice the mid, then the finish. Then a sip of water. You can make an evening out of two ounces without feeling shortchanged. The heart prefers that, and so do your better thoughts. A rush is a kind of blindness. Slow is a kind of sight. POSTURE AND THE CHAIR We don't sit around tables. We sit in chairs. That's not just a line; it's a cardiovascular strategy. A good chair with support under you and a back behind you tells your body to stop bracing. The chair in a decent lounge has weight and angle. Your feet find the floor. Your back finds the back. Your shoulders sink an inch. Every muscle that stops pretending to be a wall frees your heart from the order to hold the line. If you've ever noticed your pulse jump when you're on your feet arguing, and drop when you're seated listening, you've felt this in real time. If the chair fights you, fix it. A small cushion under your low back. A footstool if you're short. Move the ashtray so you're not twisting sideways every two minutes. The rule is simple: take one minute at the start to make the next sixty easier on your body. It sounds fussy until you try it, and then you realize comfort is not a luxury; it's the condition that makes patience possible. WARMTH, VESSELS, AND THE HONEST GLOW A good hearth throws gentle heat. Whiskey carries a version of that in the glass. A small pour can bring a sense of

warmth that spreads without shouting, especially if you're not drinking on an empty stomach. That warmth shows up in the skin and, for most people, in a sense of letting go. It's not a license to pour deep. It's a reminder that small amounts often do more of what you wanted than large ones. Your vessels respond to warmth and to calm. You don't need a second or third drink to get the message through. On cold nights, the lounge itself is part of the story. The single humidor breathes cedar into the room. The air is not rushed. You take your jacket off because the room holds you. Your heart notices. Picture the opposite: bright noise, cold wind, head down, hurry up. Same number of minutes, different cost. The hearth version is the one the heart prefers. FOOD, SALT, WATER If you want your heart to enjoy the hour, give it something decent to run on. Salt, fat, and water are the quiet team that decides whether your evening lands well. Salt without water is trouble. Fat without fiber is trouble later. Water without food makes the pour louder than it needs to be. Fix it by keeping it simple. A small plate with something salty, something with a little fat, and something fresh. Olives and almonds. Cheese and apple. Jerky and a handful of grapes. If you're watching salt for your own reasons, choose the fresh and the unsalted. Nobody gets a trophy for ignoring simple fixes. Water is the cheapest upgrade you can buy. Put a glass on the table and make a game of it: drink water whenever you change topics, or whenever someone new sits down, or whenever you set your cigar down to rest. Your palate sharpens. Your head clears. Your heart doesn't have to beat against the kind of dry that thickens the night. Add a slice of lemon if it makes you feel like you're doing more, even though the truth is you've already done the important part just by having the glass. COMPANY: THE HEART'S QUIET MEDICINE Loneliness is loud. It turns every small problem into a big one. The heart hears it. Company is quieter and kinder. A lounge is a place where company is easy. You don't have to perform. You can belong without theater. That sense of belonging is not sentimental fluff. It's a signal. It tells your body that the watch can relax and the gate can rest on the hinges. Laughter is not just noise; it changes breathing and posture and the way your chest moves. People who've worked all day at different jobs can sit in the same chairs and make each other lighter without solving a single world problem. There is a habit here worth learning: ask a real question early in the hour. "What are you smoking?" counts, but so does "How's your week, really?" The tone you set with one honest question is the tone your heart will live in for the next sixty minutes. It is hard to be tense while you listen. It is hard to be lonely while you share. If the room gives you a chance to be kind, take it. If it gives you a chance to accept kindness, take that too. Your heart prefers both roles to being a solo act. THE RISK SIDE, SAID PLAIN Cigars are smoke. Whiskey is alcohol. Both carry risk. You don't get to wish that away because you like the taste. What you do get to do is set the dials where the benefits of ritual and calm and company outweigh the costs of the leaf and the pour. That happens when you keep the amounts modest, the pace slow, the water steady, the food present, the nights finite, and the bedtime respected. It happens when you don't inhale, when you choose a cigar whose strength matches your plan for sleep, when you decide before you walk in what you'll drink and you stick to it. If you have heart questions with your doctor, ask them. No book replaces a conversation with the person who knows your numbers and your medications. If you're on something that doesn't play well with alcohol, keep the glass for the nose and the story, or skip it and keep the cigar and the company. If you're working on blood pressure, give the late-night sessions a rest and keep the hour earlier and the cigar milder. Make grown choices. The lounge will still like you. WALKING IT IN, WALKING IT OUT The heart likes movement more than it likes speeches about movement. A simple trick: build a walk into the ritual. Park a block away on purpose. Take the long lap around the building before you go in. When you're done, take a

five-minute stroll under whatever sky you've got. You are telling your body that this hour lives in the middle of a lived day, not as a bubble that nothing else touches. The walk before settles you; the walk after tells your system we are returning to normal life. Your sleep will thank you for the small bookends. If you've got a friend who likes to talk and walk, invite them to do it after the ash is cool. The conversation that started in chairs will often get better in motion. Your shoulders will know the difference. Your heart will too. You don't need a smartwatch to measure it, but if you have one, check it out of curiosity. You'll likely see what your chest already felt: a little drop in the idle speed and a smoother road. THE QUIET NUMBERS I like numbers because they make people honest, not because they make people clever. If you keep a little notebook in your pocket or a note on your phone, add a line for the heart. Write the time you started and finished, whether you ate, and how you felt. If you have a cuff at home for blood pressure and you're interested, take a reading an hour before and again an hour after on a day when you're not chasing anything. Don't chase a single number. Look at the pattern across weeks. Ask whether the ritual helps you feel calmer and kinder on average. Ask whether earlier hours make a difference. Ask whether water changes the next morning. The point is not to build a lab. It's to know yourself well enough to steer. SLEEP AND THE RED LINE Your heart does repair at night. If the ritual is stealing from sleep, you're undermining the benefit you were trying to build. Put a line in the sand. If you need to be up at six, you don't start the hour at eleven. You start it at eight and you're done by nine thirty, with a buffer after. Buffers are magic. Brush your teeth. Put the ashtray out of sight. Put the glass in the sink. Step outside for thirty seconds and let the air reset your senses. Then go to bed. You do not have to be perfect. You do have to be consistent enough that your body learns what to expect. If you hate rules, think of this as a shop practice. You don't skip eye protection because you got away with it yesterday. You don't run a saw without a guard because you're in a hurry. The small disciplines are how you earn the freedom to enjoy the work for years. The heart is the same. A bedtime is a guard. A buffer is eye protection. Use them so you can keep loving what you love. CHOOSING GENTLER WHEN GENTLER IS SMART If your week was heavy and your sleep is short, pick a smaller, gentler cigar and a lower-proof pour or no pour at all. You are not "wasting the night." You are matching the tool to the job. A creamy, medium stick will let your breath do what it needs to do. A glass of water with ice can carry all the same motions and half the same smells if you set it next to an open bottle and let your nose do the remembering. The heart will notice the difference in load and thank you in the morning. People sometimes talk as if strength is a virtue in itself. It isn't. Suitability is the virtue. A strong cigar that turns your night into a wrestling match didn't do you any favors. A high-proof pour that shouts over every other flavor and makes your sleep stumble is not a prize. Being honest about what you need tonight, and choosing the shapes that fit, is the kind of grown-up pleasure that keeps the ritual yours instead of you being its. — THE HUMIDOR AS A LESSON There is one humidor in my place, and it teaches the best lesson. It is big enough to hold what matters and small enough to demand choices. Your heart would like you to run your life the same way. Enough, not everything.

Quality, not quantity. A selection you can understand and maintain, not a warehouse that manages you. People ruin their pulse chasing more. They save it choosing better. Walk into the humidor like you mean it. Read the shelves. Pay attention to what you liked last week and why. Pick something that suits the hour you're building, not the hour you wish you had time for. The humidor also teaches care. You don't prop the door open while you browse. You go in, you choose, you close it. Keep the moisture where it belongs. The heart is like that. Hold your calm and don't prop the door open for every bit of noise the world tries to push through. Choose what gets your attention. Close the door. Sit down. Breathe. The

point isn't to live in a bubble. The point is to know when to be in the room and when to guard the threshold. THE BLUE-COLLAR HEART Workdays are real. They come with ladders and deadlines and bosses and customers and the kind of little frictions that make the chest tight by lunchtime. The blue-collar heart needs a place where it can remember it's not just a machine. The lounge is that place for a lot of us. We know each other's jobs. We know each other's luck. We know who had a good day and who needs a good ear. If you want to see an honest cardiovascular intervention, watch a guy walk in with shoulders like a coat rack and leave an hour later looking like he put the coat back where it belongs. You can help that happen for other people. Save the good chair for the late regular who limps a little. Offer the pour before they ask. Ask about their daughter's tryouts without making it a performance. Hearts like to carry other hearts for a minute. It reminds them they're not alone. That helps the numbers in ways no chart will show you, but your chest will understand. ALCOHOL, TRUTH, AND DOSE A small pour is a tool. A large pour is a decision you may or may not be happy about later. You don't need me to preach. You know the difference in your bones. If the pour helps you slow down, smell deeper, and talk better, it's doing the job. If it speeds you up, dulls your senses, and makes you chase your own tail, it's not. You can set rules that work: one pour, no refills; or two half pours with a long distance between; or water only on weeknights; or no alcohol when the next day is a heavy one. Make a rule you respect and tell a friend so they can respect it with you. You don't need anyone to police you. You do need to be honest. For some folks the rule is no alcohol at all. That is not a downgrade. That is a smart plan that leaves the ritual intact. The cigar, the breath, the chair, the talk—those are doing most of the work anyway. A ginger ale with ice looks right in the light and carries just fine between stories. If you are the guy who stays dry and still shows up, you are doing your heart and your friendships a favor at the same time. MEDICINE, DOCTORS, AND STRAIGHT TALK If you take something for blood pressure, or you've had a heart scare, or your doctor gave you marching orders, honor that conversation. Bring the ritual to the plan, not the other way around. Ask your doctor how to time your evenings. Ask whether there are red flags to watch for. Ask whether your plan for small, slow, and early makes sense for you. You are not asking permission to misbehave. You are asking for how to keep your good things inside your good life. If you have a cuff at home, learn to use it right. Sit, feet flat, back supported, arm at heart level. Rest five minutes. Then read. Do it at the same times on a few different days and see the pattern. Don't panic about one high number or brag about one low one. Patterns are what matter. If the ritual helps the pattern, you're on the right road. If it hurts it, adjust the dials: earlier, gentler, less often, more water, more walking, more sleep. — THE FIRE WITHOUT THE FRENZY Everyone knows a guy who thinks heat equals good. He torches the foot like he's trying to weld it shut. He knocks back a pour like he's racing a commercial break. His heart is along for that ride whether it wants to be or not. Don't be that guy. The fire is in the flavor and the conversation, not in the speed. Toast the foot with patience. Let the cherry find its balance. Sip like you're reading a letter, not paying a bill. The frenzy costs you more than it buys. If you catch yourself speeding up because the story got exciting, take a breath and a sip of water and let the flavors catch back up to you. Your heart will do the same. The best nights have arcs the way good songs do. They start quiet, build in the middle, then settle with something true. You want your pulse to ride that kind of curve, not a square wave of jabs and jumps. You can steer that on purpose if you want to. It's not control for control's sake. It's the craft of living.

THE CHECKLIST THAT WORKS

This is the one I keep taped in my head: Before: Eat something. Drink water. Set a stop time. Decide the pour or no pour. Pick a cigar that matches the hour and the bedtime. During: Breathe slow. Pace the puff. Sip small. Water between. Talk and listen. Aim your smoke. Mind your posture. Laugh when it comes. After: Put it out before it turns bitter. Stop while the story has a good last line. Clean the ashtray. Rinse the glass. Step into the night for a minute. Walk a block. Sleep. You can adjust that to your life. The point isn't to be a monk. The point is to build a habit that keeps paying you back. Your heart likes routines it can trust. Give it one. A WORD ABOUT AGE AND STRENGTH As we get older, the margin gets narrower. The same cigar that used to be a friendly weight can feel like a workout on a short night. The same pour that once felt like courage can feel like clutter. That's not loss; that's information. Adjust. Trade a powerhouse for a medium that tastes like bread and cream and lets your breath do most of the good. Trade proof for flavor. Trade late for early. Trade quantity for gratitude. You will not miss what you think you will. You will notice that the hour shows you more when you stop yelling at it. THE HEARTH AND THE JOBSITE A lot of this chapter is about the chairs, but the results show up at work. The heart that got an honest hour at the hearth carries that steadiness to the jobsite. You climb the ladder with rhythm. You handle the customer who's had a day without borrowing their panic. You finish the list without feeding the part of you that thinks lists are the point of life. The hearth is not an escape. It is a way you practice being the person you like being when the world is noisy. The heart keeps that practice longer than the smoke keeps the room. If you've ever had a run of weeks where you skipped the ritual and found yourself sharp with people who didn't deserve it, you know the cost. The lounge is not a band-aid. It's a rehearsal space for calm. Your heart learns what you teach it, and it teaches it back to you at noon on a job that has nothing to do with cigars or whiskey. That is a benefit you can feel without a chart or a study. It is a better day made out of better hours. — THE LAST FIVE MINUTES Don't ruin the ending. The last inches of a cigar are honest and darker. If the flavors turn bitter, set it down. Quit while the memory is sweet. Let the last sips be water. People remember the end of things. Your heart does too. If you make a habit of clean endings, your nervous system will start looking forward to them instead of arguing. When you drive away, drive slow for the first block. Look at the sky if it's there to be seen. The hearth hour is over, but the heart hour is still echoing. Let it. THE SHORT PRAYER I don't put many prayers in print, but here's one that works whether you use that word or not. Before you light, give yourself ten seconds. "May this hour make me calmer, kinder, and more grateful. May I leave better than I arrived." You don't need anyone's permission to ask for that. The asking itself changes the hour. The heart hears it. So do the people across from you even if you never say it out loud. You become the kind of person who builds hours that make other people's hearts feel a little safer. That's the best benefit there is. THE HEARTH INSIDE THE CHEST If this chapter had to be one sentence, it would be this: build a hearth your heart can carry when you stand up. The cigar is a tool for breath. The pour is a tool for pace. The chair is a tool for posture. The company is a tool for belonging. Put them together with attention and boundaries and you get a small, sturdy practice that makes

tomorrow better without pretending to fix the world. You don't have to argue about it. You just have to do it. The proof is in the way your chest feels when you climb the steps to your door and in the way you say hello to your people when you walk in. The heart and the hearth want the same things: warmth, steadiness, and a sense that the work matters. Give them that, and they will give you the kind of benefit that shows up where it counts—in the shape of your days, in the way you listen, in the way you sleep, in the way you carry yourself when the world tries to borrow your pulse. That is not a miracle. It is just good craft, learned slowly and kept on purpose. So light carefully. Sip modestly. Sit well. Breathe. Laugh. Thank the room and the people and your own stubborn heart for carrying you. Then go home steady. Tomorrow will bring its noise. You'll bring your hearth.

CHAPTER 5

Stress Relief, Mindfulness, and Mental Health

This chapter is about the part you can feel in your chest but can't hold in your hands. We talk a lot about flavor and craft, but none of that matters much if your mind is running hot and your nerves are a live wire. Stress is not a character flaw; it's a load. The question is whether your rituals lighten the load or add to it. A cigar and a modest pour can be tools for steadying yourself—if you aim them right. Not magic. Not medicine. Just tools you can use to give your mind a place to stand while the day stops shaking. WHAT STRESS REALLY DOES Stress is the body asking, "Are we safe?" and not getting a clean answer. The heart idles high. The breath gets short and shallow. The jaw tightens. The shoulders float. The brain starts seeing problems behind every ordinary corner. The trouble is not that stress exists; you need it to sprint, think fast, and stay sharp when it counts. The trouble is when the dial gets stuck on high long after the danger is gone. Most of us aren't running from fires. We're running from emails, bills, traffic, and the grind of being responsible for people we love. That's still a load. It just responds to different tools than sprinting does. The cigar-and-chair hour helps because it reverses the signals. Your breath gets longer. Your posture stops pretending to be a brick wall. The pace of the evening becomes a metronome for your thoughts. The glass doesn't do the work; the ritual does. If you build the hour like a craft—deliberate, simple, paced—you create the conditions where stress can stop shouting and start clearing out. THE THREE LEVERS: BREATH, PACE, ATTENTION There are only three levers you can pull on purpose without special gear. Breath is first. Pace is second. Attention is third. If you learn to pull all three, you can change your head without running ten miles or buying anything. Breath is the clutch. You don't have to know the vocabulary to feel the gear change when you go slow in and slower out. You light the cigar and you watch the cherry bloom. You draw gently. You wait. You exhale fully. Count if you want: in for four, out for six. The numbers aren't sacred. The longer exhale is. It tells your body the watchman can take a break. Pace is the calendar. A cigar punishes hurry. Your nervous system is the same way. If you teach yourself to live at the speed of a clean burn line, you're teaching your body to trust the next minute. A small pour sipped like a letter— read, considered, set down—fits the same rhythm. The hour becomes a steady lane instead of a sprint and a stop and a sprint again. Attention is the steering. Stress throws your focus like gravel under the tires. Ritual gives you something to drive toward. "I'm going to notice the first third." "I'm going to find the finish on this pour." "I'm going to ask Joe about his son's construction job and actually listen." These are small promises you can keep. The mind obeys promises that are close to the ground. THE MINDFULNESS YOU ALREADY KNOW HOW TO DO

People hear "mindfulness" and picture a mat or a bottle of scented oil. You don't need either. You already know how to be mindful because you've fixed things with your hands. You look closely. You use the right pressure. You finish clean. Do the same with your hour. Set the scene. Put your phone face down and out of reach. Choose a chair that holds you. Angle the ashtray so you don't twist to use it. Put water on the table. Look at the cigar like you look at a piece of wood before you cut it— grain, color, condition. Look at the pour like you look at a tool before you pick it up—clean, ready, the right one for the job. Light with patience. Toast the foot like you're warming a stubborn bolt—steady heat, small turns, no melting. When the smoke arrives, don't grab at it. Let it come to you. Put the glass to your nose and learn what it wants to say before you tell it anything. The mindful part is not fancy. It is paying attention without hurrying. THE TALK THAT HEALS A lounge isn't a therapist's office, but it can be a place where honest talk shows up without name tags. "How's work?" is small talk. "How's work, really?" is an open door. Most men don't get many doors. When a room makes it normal to tell the truth in small pieces, the pressure drops. You don't need to solve anyone's life. You need to listen like a neighbor and tell your own story without turning it into a speech. Stress hates daylight. Let a little in. There are simple habits that make this easier. Ask one real question in the first ten minutes. Put away the story you were waiting to tell and ask someone else how their week actually went. When someone gives you detail, don't rush to fix it. Nod. Ask the next simple question. Let people finish their thought. Your nervous system settles when you give your attention instead of guarding it. If you tend to keep everything inside, use the cigar as your timer. "I'll tell one honest thing before the first ash falls." Not a confession. Not a performance. Just a real sentence that took a little courage to say. Your mood isn't a pothole to be patched; it's a road that gets better when more wheels share it. ALCOHOL AND MOOD—THE TRUTH ABOUT DOSE There's a straight line between dose and mood, and it's not always your friend. A small pour can round the edges off a noisy day. Two small pours can make you looser and kinder. Three can turn the hour into a blur that borrows tomorrow's good feelings. Four will bill you with interest. This is not a sermon; it's a map. If the point of the evening is to feel steadier, keep the glass in the range where flavors sharpen and talk deepens. More than that and you're chasing a feeling that won't stay chased. If you've had rough patches with alcohol, or you're on medicine that doesn't play well with it, the fix is simple: keep the ritual and skip the pour. Ginger ale and ice look right in a rocks glass. Club soda with a twist opens the nose and keeps your head clear. The cigar and the chair do most of the work anyway. You won't be missing as much as you think. WHAT TO DO ON ANXIETY NIGHTS Some nights the mind doesn't want to sit. It runs laps in a room you can't see. Anxiety loves speed and prediction. Your job is to deny it both. Slow breath. Slow pace. No forecasts. You cut the cap clean. You toast patiently. You let the first inch be nothing but rhythm: puff, wait, exhale, water, wait. Don't start big topics until your chest matches the burn line. If your thoughts sprint ahead to tomorrow's problems, aim your attention at small details in the room: the humidor door hinge, the pattern in the ash, the way the light catches a bottle label. It's not avoidance. It's traction. If the runaway feeling doesn't let up, stand up and take a short walk outside. Feel the air. Name five things you can see. Name four you can feel. Three you can hear. Two you can smell. One you can taste. This old grounding trick works because it makes the brain use the present instead of the future. When you come back to the chair, the cigar will be where you left it. So will your hour. WHAT TO DO ON LOW DAYS Some days are flat. You're not on fire; you're out of gas. A heavy cigar will turn that into a job. Choose gentle and

flavorful. Cream and bread notes do more for a tired mind than pepper and asphalt. Keep the pour small or skip it. Eat something. The goal of a low day hour isn't to climb a mountain. It's to put your feet on steady ground. Talk if you can. Sit quiet if you can't. Let the room carry you. If you're riding a long streak of these days—two weeks or more where the light doesn't come on—see a professional. That's not weakness. That's a tool like any other. ANGER, AND HOW TO NOT FEED IT Anger can be clean or it can be poison. Clean anger stands up for something and then sits back down. Poison anger mutters while you sleep and wakes up with you in the morning. Don't bring poison anger to the lounge. If you have to, create rules for yourself. Don't light until you can say what you're mad about without spitting. Don't drink when your first thought is "I deserve it" or "I earned this" after a fight. Those are red flags, not celebrations. Choose a cigar that keeps you busy with flavor and a pace that keeps your mouth from racing. When you feel your voice getting sharp, stop, drink water, look at the ash. The goal is not to be a saint. It's to stop the hour from turning into fuel. GRIEF IN A CHAIR Grief is not a problem to fix. It's a weight to carry long enough that your legs get strong. A lounge can be a safe place to sit with it. People don't expect speeches. Nobody asks you to smile. You light, you breathe, you say the name when you're ready. The right company knows how to sit quiet and let the smoke fill the words you don't have yet. If you cry, you're in a room with ashtrays and Kleenex. No one will die of seeing you be human. When the hour ends, you walk out a little less alone. That matters more than clever advice. — THE NOTEBOOK THAT HELPS You don't need a journal to be a person, but a pocket notebook can keep you honest and teach you what works. One page per night. Write the cigar, the bottle (or "water"), the start time, the end time, and three short lines: "Before,"

"During," "After." Before: two words for the mood you

carried in. During: one thing you noticed—flavor, talk, the

way the room sounded. After: two words for the mood you

carried out. You will see patterns. Maybe early nights beat

late nights. Maybe water every two minutes makes you feel

smarter tomorrow. Maybe you always walk out kinder

when you ask one true question in the first ten minutes.

That's not a therapy plan. That's a craft log for your head.

THE FIVE-MINUTE RESET Some nights you need a

ritual but you don't have an hour. Use a five-minute

version that still speaks your brain's language. Step outside.

Put your phone in your pocket. Breathe in for four, out for

six, ten times. Say out loud what worked today. Say out

loud what you're worried about tomorrow. Promise

yourself one small action you'll take in the morning. Then

walk back in. If you have a cigar, save it for when you can

pay attention to it. The point is to reset, not to rush.

MINDFUL PAIRINGS (A CLASSROOM FOR YOUR NERVES) Pairing is education if you make it that way. Pick one simple goal for the night and measure it with your senses. "Does vanilla in the whiskey make the toast in the cigar speak up?" "Does pepper in the retrohale pull orange out of the glass?" "Does a creamy cigar round off a high-proof pour's sharp parts?" Write down what you find. It doesn't matter if you're "right." You're teaching your brain to hold a thread while the rest of life tries to yank it away. That practice shows up later when you're trying to listen to your kid's story while the dishwasher complains. BREATH DRILLS THAT DON'T FEEL LIKE DRILLS There's a simple pattern that fits the hour: box breathing without the box. Draw. Wait. Exhale. Wait. Repeat. If you want numbers: 4-2-6-2. Four seconds in. Two still. Six out. Two still. That "still" is the part many people miss. It tells the body you're not in a footrace. Do this during the first inch and anytime the conversation gets spicy. Your head stays clear. Your voice stays warm. When you go home, you'll be able to find the same rhythm in the quiet and use it without the cigar.

BOREDOM, RESTLESSNESS, AND THE GENTLE FIX Sometimes the problem isn't stress; it's the low hum of boredom that makes you pick up your phone and lose half the night to nothing. The fix is small and silly: give yourself a task. Build a flavor map on a napkin. Sketch the burn line every half-inch and write one word next to each segment. Or set a timer for three minutes and see how many nosing notes you can name without repeating. Games like that seem childish until you notice you put the phone away for an hour and felt like a person again. KEEPING THE RITUAL HUMBLE Ritual goes wrong when it becomes a performance. The cigar and the glass are not a costume. They aren't armor. They're tools for building a quiet place. Keep them humble and they'll keep you honest. If you feel yourself reaching for the rarest bottle because the day was bad, stop. If you feel yourself reaching for the strongest cigar because your pride was hurt, stop. Switch to water. Switch to gentle. Switch to talk. You don't have to prove anything to earn an hour of peace.

BOUNDARIES THAT MAKE THE HOUR BETTER A boundary is a kindness you give yourself in advance. A few good ones: • One cigar. Let it be enough. • One small pour, or two half pours far apart, or none. • Water between sips. • Food before or during. • A start time that respects sleep. • A stop time you actually keep. • No phone in hand. • No big decisions in the last inch. • If the talk turns mean, call it and reset. These aren't rules to win points with anyone. They're guardrails so the hour does what it's supposed to do: make you steadier and kinder when you stand up. WHEN TO SKIP THE RITUAL Wisdom sometimes says "not tonight." If you're sick, sleep. If you're driving, keep your glass a nose and a taste or skip it. If you're on a new medicine and you don't know how it plays with alcohol, don't test it in a lounge. If you're grieving hard and the room will turn into a performance, take a walk with a friend instead. If you had three rough nights in a row, put two dry ones on the calendar, and fill them with the same chair, the same water, and maybe a book. The point of a ritual is to help you live. If it can't do that tonight, bench it and try again later. HOW TO HELP SOMEONE ELSE IN THE ROOM Mental health isn't just a solo sport. Pay attention to the guys who show up quieter than usual. You don't need a speech. Sit next to them. Offer a light. Ask a soft question. Listen twice as much as you talk. If someone's pouring too fast, set your water down where they can see it and say, "I'm pacing tonight." People follow small examples more than big lectures. If someone tells you they're really struggling, offer the next step—a drive home, a check-in tomorrow, the name of a counselor who helped you once. If you think someone might hurt themselves, take it seriously. Stay with them. In the U.S., you can call or text

988 for immediate help. There's no honor in pretending it's fine when it isn't. BLUE-COLLAR MINDFULNESS Mindfulness sounds fancy until you watch a welder. Full attention, steady hands, patience, clean finish—that's mindfulness. You already know how to do it; you just learned it at work instead of on a cushion. The lounge is the same classroom with softer lights. Commit to the task in front of you. Don't rush. Respect the materials. Clean up after yourself. Say thanks. Those habits change your head more than any slogan can. THE SMALL PRAYER

I don't write many prayers into a book like this, but here's one that doesn't need religion to work: "May this hour make me calmer, kinder, and more grateful. May I leave better than I arrived." Say it out loud or under your breath. The point is to aim your heart before you light. If you start there, the rest tends to follow. WHAT TO DO WHEN THE OLD TRICKS STOP WORKING Every ritual gets stale if you never change the angle. If the hour feels flat, change one variable. New chair. New time of day. New company. New cigar size—robusto instead of toro. New glass—rye instead of bourbon, or water instead of anything. Bring a notebook and decide to write three sentences you haven't written before. Volunteer to be the one who offers the light. Work the humidor for the new guy. Fresh air moves the same smoke. SLEEP, DREAMS, AND THE MORNING AFTER Good sleep is mental health you can't fake. If the ritual steals from sleep, it steals from the rest of your life. Start earlier. Keep it gentler. Water heavy at the end. Leave a buffer between the last puff and the pillow. Wash your hands and face so the nose doesn't carry the hour to bed. Open a window for a minute. The goal is to let the nervous system know the show is over. If you dream weird after a heavy night, that's a sign you don't like the dose, not a sign dreams are the enemy. Adjust. Keep the ritual serving the morning, not robbing it. THE CHECKLIST THAT SAVES BAD DAYS Keep this in your head or on a card: Before: Eat something. Pour small or skip. Water on the table. Phone away. Start time set. During: Breathe slow. Pace the puff. Water between. Listen more than you talk. Notice one new flavor. Ask one real question. After: Stop while the story is sweet. Clean up. Step outside for air. Ten slow breaths. Go home. Sleep. You don't need perfection. You need consistency. The brain loves knowing what comes next, and the heart loves not being surprised. — A WORD ON PROFESSIONAL HELP Everything I've said so far lives in the lane of ordinary human load. If you're carrying more than that—panic that pins you, sadness that doesn't lift for weeks, thoughts about hurting yourself, or trouble with alcohol that keeps winning—use the tools that are built for heavier jobs. Talk to your doctor. Find a counselor. Tell a friend and let them drive you if that's what it takes. In the U.S., call or text 988 if you're in crisis. None of that cancels your chair or your humidor. It just keeps you here to enjoy them longer. THE HOUR AS PRACTICE Think of your hour like the way athletes think of drills. You're training breath, pace, and attention so that the rest of your week gets easier. When a hard conversation shows up at work, you'll already know how to breathe slow and listen. When a long drive stacks up, you'll already know how to pace and sip water. When the news shouts, you'll already know how to pick the one thing worth your focus. Practice is how the brain learns. The cigar and the chair are just a good place to sneak the practice in. THE STORY YOU'RE WRITING One more thing: you're building a story about yourself while you do all this. "I'm someone who keeps my word to myself." "I'm someone who can calm a room." "I'm someone who knows when to stop." Those are better stories than "I deserve" or "I need" or "I can't help it." The glass and the smoke are symbols you can read differently depending on the night. Read them as tools, not demands. Read them as a way to say thank you for getting through the day. Read them as proof you can make a small, beautiful thing out of an ordinary evening. THE LAST LIGHT

Endings matter. Put the cigar down before the bitterness starts shouting. Let the last taste be clean water. Say goodnight to the room. Walk to your car slower than you came in. Notice the air. Check the stars if they're there. Call it a win if you made the hour gentle and honest. Then go home and be the person you practiced being while the smoke lifted and the glass caught the light. You don't need a miracle to help your mind. You need an hour built on purpose. Breath, pace, attention. A chair that fits. Company that tells the truth kindly. Water on the table. Boundaries you respect. That's the shape. Build it as often as you can and protect it when you have to. The rest of your life will thank you in ways no book can measure. So tonight, light with care. Sip with respect. Listen. Laugh. Let the hour be enough. Let tomorrow find you steadier because you chose

to be present for one small piece of your own life.

CHAPTER 6

Whiskey and Cigar Pairings: An Art and a Science

Pairing whiskey and cigars is one of the friendliest arguments in the lounge. Everyone has a favorite. Everyone has a story. Some folks swear by a single bottle for every stick; others change lanes like a DJ. Underneath all that opinion is a simple goal: let the cigar and the whiskey make each other taste more like themselves, not less. If the pour gets flatter or the cigar turns harsh, the pairing missed. When it works, flavors line up and take turns: nose, sip, finish; toast, draw, retrohale. You will know because the room goes quiet in a good way. This chapter gives you both sides of the craft. The science – how sweetness, proof, oak, and spice interact with smoke – and the art – how to choose for season, mood, and company without turning the night into homework. You do not need flashcards. You need a feel for three dials (intensity, sweetness, spice), a short map of whiskey families and cigar lanes, and a handful of plays that travel anywhere. THE PALATE, IN PLAIN LANGUAGE Taste is smell plus texture plus temperature plus the little nerves that decide whether something feels warm, sharp, or cool. Whiskey brings sweetness from grain and barrel (vanillin, caramelized wood sugars), bitter from tannin and char, spice from rye content and toasted oak, and heat from ethanol. Cigars bring natural sweetness from cured leaf, mild bitterness and earth from alkaloids, umami from roasted notes, and spice from seed and soil – especially in the retrohale. Put the two together and you are mixing chemistry with cadence. Heat opens aroma. Water unlocks flavor. Pace decides whether the oils in the cigar caramelize or burn. The mouth notices when you behave. Aromatics matter more than most of us admit. A pour with orange-peel brightness will lift a nutty Sumatra. A cigar with cocoa in the middle will pull chocolate out of a sherry-finished Scotch. If you want an easy win, think like a cook: salt brightens, fat smooths, acid lifts, sweet rounds. Nuts, cheese, chocolate, and water are not snacks here; they are small tools. THE THREE DIALS Intensity (volume). Loud, medium, quiet. A delicate Connecticut will fold under a barrel-strength showboat. A dark Broadleaf will not wake up for a whispering Irish unless you give it a reason. Match volume first; break the rule later on purpose. Sweetness. Vanilla, caramel, honey, dried fruit. Sweetness is the shock absorber; it smooths edges and balances pepper. Too much turns syrupy and hides detail. Spice. Two families: baking spice (cinnamon, clove, nutmeg) and sharp spice (black pepper, rye bite). Baking spice comforts; sharp spice wakes. Both are good. The question is what the cigar already brings and whether you want harmony or contrast. Get those three right and you can wander anywhere with confidence. Miss them and you will start editing your experience with excuses. A quiet reminder: if you say "it gets better after ten minutes," you probably matched intensity wrong or you are rushing. WHISKEY FAMILIES (WORKING MAP)

Bourbon (corn-led). - Classic or low-rye: caramel, vanilla, corn bread, soft oak. Friendly with toast and cream. - High-rye: more orange peel, pepper, and snap. Loves nutty cigars and anything that needs backbone. - Wheated: round, pastry-sweet; great with Connecticut and gentle Habanos. - Barrel proof: concentrated flavor plus heat; almost always better with water. Rye. - 95 percent rye brings pepper, spearmint, citrus, and sometimes dill; lower-rye "barely legal" styles feel like spicy bourbons. - Rye is the best friend of creamy sticks – it keeps them awake without picking a fight. Scotch. - Ex-bourbon Speyside or Highland: pear, apple, vanilla, clean oak. Great with shade wrappers and toasty Habanos. - Sherry finish: raisins, walnut, baking spice. Built for maduros with cocoa. - Peated or Islay: maritime smoke, iodine, black pepper. Pair with earthy Broadleaf or rich Nicaraguan blends and give bedtime some thought. Irish. - Pot-still and malt styles bring honey, biscuit, orchard fruit, and a silky texture. Ideal for lighter cigars, early evenings, and kindness. American single malt / Japanese / Canadian. - Lean malts echo ex-bourbon Scotch but with American wood; Japanese often chase balance and tea-like clarity; Canadian blends are soft and grain-forward. Treat all three like a lane: gentle to medium body; often great with Cameroon, Sumatra, or light Habano. CIGAR LANES (WORKING MAP) Connecticut Shade (USA or Ecuador). Cream, toast, hay, a little vanilla. Quiet elegance. Habano (Cuban-seed grown widely). Toast, warm spice, cedar, sometimes citrus peel. Corojo. Red pepper, cedar, dry sweetness; stronger personality. Sumatra (Indonesia or Ecuador). Nutmeg, tea, sandalwood, faint molasses; interesting without being bossy. San Andres (Mexico). Earth and cocoa; sturdy; great binder too. Broadleaf (USA). Chocolate, espresso, molasses, earth; cool burn if you respect the pace. Cameroon (Africa). Baking spice, ginger, nuttiness; fragile but lovely. Maduro (process, not species). Darker fermentation; sweetness rises; strength depends on the bunch, not the color. If you would rather not memorize names, sort cigars by body (light, medium, full) and lean (sweet-cocoa, nut-bread, pepper-earth, cream-toast). That is enough to steer the glass. THE PAIRING FRAMEWORK (NO GRID REQUIRED) 1) Pick a whiskey lane (sweet, spicy, fruit and nut, smoke, clean malt). 2) Pick a cigar lane (cream and toast, nut and bread, cocoa and coffee, spice and earth). 3) Decide complement (like with like) or contrast (opposites that cooperate). 4) Match intensity or support the louder partner with water, food, or pace. 5) Set the rhythm: nose -> sip -> wait -> draw -> wait -> water -> talk. 6) Listen to the chair. If your shoulders drop and your voice softens, you are in bounds. TWELVE RELIABLE PAIRINGS (WHY THEY WORK) 1) Connecticut Shade + Wheated Bourbon Cream and pastry notes meet vanilla and caramel. Almonds and apple slices on the side make it sing. Pace slow; let toast become bread. 2) Connecticut Shade +

Ex-Bourbon Malt Pear and honey with toast and hay. Elegant, almost tea-like. A small twist of lemon over the glass can lift aroma without changing the liquid.

3) Light Habano + Pot-Still Irish Warm toast and gentle spice with honey and biscuit. If "weeknight comfort" was a pairing, this is it. Cheddar and green apple help the finish stay tidy.

4) Medium Habano + 95-Proof Rye Cedar and baking spice meet orange peel and clove. Pepper behaves. Salty cashews keep sweetness in check.

5) Sumatra + High-Rye Bourbon Nutmeg and tea leaf find citrus and oak. A classic complement and contrast hybrid; subtle and talkative at once.

6) Cameroon + Sherried Scotch Baking spice and ginger with raisin and walnut. If you like dessert without sugar, this is your lane. One square of dark chocolate (70 percent) is the chorus.

7) San Andres Maduro + Ex-Bourbon Malt Earth and cocoa set against vanilla and clean oak. Perfect when you want weight without smoke-on-smoke drama.

8) Broadleaf Maduro + Sherried Scotch Chocolate and espresso with dried fruit and nut. Add water to the Scotch until the fruit stands up; the cigar will carry the bass.

9) Broadleaf Maduro + Peated Malt Maritime smoke with earth and coffee. Start with small sips and a glass of water. Respect bedtime and neighbors.

10) Sweet-Core Nicaraguan (Maduro) + Barrel-Proof Bourbon Big oak with big body. Water is not optional; a few drops bring flavor forward and heat back. Toasted pecans are the right snack.

11) Corojo + Classic Bourbon (low-rye) Red pepper and cedar with caramel and vanilla. Think campfire

and cornbread. Add a drop of honey if the cigar is aggressive; strange, but it works.

12) Spice-Forward Nicaraguan (Habano) + Canadian or Japanese Blended Let the cigar carry the spice while the glass provides polish. Great for newcomers who want interest without wrestling. PACE MAKES THE PAIRING Light the cigar first and let the first third settle. Sip small. If you are pairing a heavy cigar with a heavy pour, reduce proof with water before the first sip. A dart of water between sips keeps the palate alive; a bite of something salty resets sweetness before it gets sticky. If the ash looks like a lightning bolt, you are racing. If the whiskey smells like only ethanol, you are racing. Slow is flavor. Retrohale is a tool, not a dare. Use a small portion once the cigar warms. If it stings your sinuses, the blend or the pace is asking for gentler handling. SEASONAL WHEEL Spring: floral

malts, young bourbons, cigars that smell like toast and morning air. Citrus at the table. Summer: lower proof, longer ice; creamy cigars that do not fight heat. Salt is the hero. Autumn: rye and sherry take the stage; nuts and cocoa find easy work. Fireside weather, inside or out. Winter: peat gets a job and maduros put on a sweater. Proof creeps up; water rides shotgun. Seasons are not rules. They are reminders that the same pairing can taste different when the trees change color. SITUATIONAL SETS Weeknight Forty-Five: short robusto with a low-proof bourbon; water first; bedtime respected.

After a Heavy Dinner: Cameroon with pot-still Irish; baking spice meets apple; cleaner finish than a dessert cart. Rainy Saturday: Broadleaf Maduro with sherried malt and a square of chocolate. Slow radio. Celebration: full Nicaraguan with barrel-proof – proof tamed, food nearby, stories without microphones. Coffee

Hour: Connecticut with ex-bourbon malt – or with coffee alone, no guilt. Company Night: three lanes on the table – wheated + Connecticut; rye + Sumatra; sherry + Maduro. Let people discover rather than lecture. COMMON MISTAKES (AND CLEAN FIXES) - Heat vs. heat: cask-strength plus pepper bomb equals nose workout. Fix: add water, slow your draw, or swap one partner. - Syrup overload: sweet bourbon and sweet Maduro with dessert and no water. Fix: salted nuts, water, and a pause. - Peat with delicate shade: cigar tastes like it went camping without permission. Fix: switch to honeyed Irish or a malt with no smoke; save peat for earthier sticks. - Proof drift: the second pour gets taller. Fix: pre-measure; smaller glass; ritualize water. - Racing: ash zigzags; whiskey noses like paint thinner. Fix: count to five between actions; set the cigar down for a minute. - Room politics: some flavor lanes are very aromatic. If the lounge is small, pick a pour that shares nicely. MYTHS THAT DESERVE RETIREMENT

"Dark wrapper means strong." Strength mostly lives in the bunch. A maduro can be gentle; a pale wrapper can hide a lion. "The wrapper is 70 percent of flavor." There is no fixed percentage that is true across blends. Wrapper, binder, and filler cooperate. "Only X pairs with Y." Rigid rules are how good nights get smaller. Lanes and dials are better than commandments. "Ice is cheating." Ice is a tool. If it helps you find flavor and pace, use it. "No water with whiskey." Water is how many flavors introduce themselves. Pride is hard on palates. A HOME FLIGHT (TEACHES FAST, COSTS LITTLE) Half-ounce pours; one cigar cut into thirds per lane (or three small cigars). Label A through E. A) Wheated bourbon + Connecticut third. B) 95-proof rye + Sumatra third. C) Ex-bourbon malt + toasty Habano third. D) Sherry-finished malt + Maduro third. E) Mild peat + earthy Broadleaf third. Rule: five-word notes only. "Toast, vanilla, easy finish." "Orange peel woke it up." "Chocolate loves raisin." Vote for Best

Complement and Best Contrast. Arguing is allowed; scorekeeping is not. HOSTING A PAIRING NIGHT (AND NOT TURNING INTO STAFF) Set a small table: water pitcher, small plates, salted nuts, apples, chocolate, clean cutters, a couple of lighters. Announce proof once: "These two are 100; this is 114 – water is right there." Pour small; keep bottles visible so people can revisit. If someone says they are done, believe them. End while the room is smiling. A great host protects tomorrow as carefully as tonight.

ADVANCED PLAYS (WHEN YOU ARE READY) Water dosing. Two drops can flip a pour from heat-forward to flavor-forward. Find the line where fruit or vanilla rises and heat sits down. Split pours. Pair a creamy cigar with two small glasses: one wheated bourbon, one rye. Move back and forth. Notice

what each emphasizes. This trains your palate faster than any chart. Finish talk. Wine casks (sherry, port, madeira) bring dried fruit and nut; they love cocoa-leaning cigars. Rum finishes tilt toward molasses and banana bread – nice with Corojo if you keep proof honest. Citrus mist. A tiny orange peel expressed over (not into) the glass can lift a nutty Sumatra without changing the liquid. Old bartender trick. Looks fancy, costs nothing. Food as tool. Salt resets sweetness. Fat smooths pepper. Acid (apple) brightens cocoa. Do not build a charcuterie tower; put a handful of each on the table and watch pairings click. NOTE-KEEPING THAT ACTUALLY GETS USED Keep a tiny log with three lines per pairing: - Cigar / glass / date. - Three words each (nose, middle, finish). - One sentence: what to change next time. Example: "Sumatra + rye, weeknight. Nose orange and cedar; middle nutmeg; finish clean. Next time: add water earlier." After a month of these, you will know your lanes better than any internet thread could tell you. THREE MINI CASE STUDIES Case 1: The Quiet Win. Tuesday. You choose a light Habano robusto and an Irish pot-still. First inch shows toast and soft nut. One ounce pour, a little water. Conversation is slow. Result: flavors take turns; you sleep on schedule; you are glad you kept it small. Lesson: weeknights love moderation and warm spice. Case 2: The Overreach. Friday. You pair a peppery Nicaraguan with cask-strength bourbon and forget water. First five minutes taste like ambition. Retrohale barks. After water and salted nuts the room calms, but you learned the expensive way. Lesson: proof is a dial, not a dare; salt and water are tools. Case 3: The Crowd Pleaser. Birthday meet-up. You set out three lanes: wheated + Connecticut; rye + Sumatra; sherry + Maduro. People vote with quiet smiles, not speeches. The rye flight goes fastest; the sherry pairing gets the most "wow." Lesson: variety makes a room smarter; your favorite will sometimes lose and that is fine. TROUBLESHOOTING, LIVE "Whiskey tastes thin suddenly." Stop. Water. Gentle draw. Oxygen helps; rushing hurts. "Cigar went bitter." You are running hot. Set it down for a full minute; relight softly; slow cadence. "Pairing is too sweet." Salted nuts or olives; a splash of water; shift to a rye lane next time. "Pairing is sharp." Two drops of water and a square of chocolate; or grab a cream-leaning cigar. "You feel sharp." Breathe. Water. Let someone else talk. The set often fixes itself once you do. THE ONE-CHAIR TEST We do not sit around tables. We sit in chairs. A pairing that only works as a performance does not work. Sit down. Nose the glass, then the room. Draw like you plan to be here a while. If the pairing lowers your shoulders and raises your attention, you hit the mark. If your jaw tightens or the retrohale stings mean, reduce proof, reduce pepper, or add a little sweetness. The chair will tell you faster than a scorecard.

QUICK MATRIX (TAPE THIS INSIDE A CABINET)

Sweet (bourbon) <-> Cream/Toast (Connecticut or Habano) Spice (rye) <-> Cream/Toast or Nut/Bread (Sumatra) Fruit/Nut (Irish or Sherry) <-> Cocoa/Coffee

(Maduro or Broadleaf) Smoke (peat) <-> Earth/Coffee (Broadleaf or Nicaragua)

Clean Malt (ex-bourbon Scotch or Japanese) <-> Connecticut/Habano/Sumatra Add water if the glass shouts. Add salt if the set gets sticky. Pace like someone who plans to sleep. A WORD ON HUMOR AND HUMILITY Pairing is not a talent show. Keep your jokes light and your advice shorter than your draw. If someone loves a combo you would not pick, let them. Their chair is doing its job. Your ego does not have to. If you want a line that keeps peace: "I get orange peel on the rye, and the Sumatra turns nutmeg for me. You?" Then stop talking and listen. CLOSING THIS CHAPTER Pairing is an art because taste is personal, and a science because patterns keep showing up when you pay attention. Learn the dials. Know your lanes. Keep water near and pride far. You will stack more good nights than bad, and the ones that miss will teach you faster than any lecture. End the night while the flavors still agree with each other. Leave a little good in the glass and a little promise in the box. Tomorrow will thank you, and so will the chair.

CHAPTER 7

The Social Ritual of the Lounge

A cigar lounge can be many things—a shop, a club, a third place—but the one in these pages is my favorite lounge. When I say "we," I mean the crew at that spot—the place where the bell dings, the host/tobacconist looks up already smiling and says it the way only family can: "Welcome home." Every lounge has its own look and rhythm. Yours might trade brick for tile or jazz for sports highlights. What follows is the room I share at my favorite place—not a universal template. Home is the word we reach for. Not because we live there, but because when we're there we live a certain way. Everyone seems to know everyone, and if you don't yet, you will by the end of the week. Names stick. Stories stick. People stick. It doesn't matter what you do for a living, how you vote, what you worship, or where your grandparents came from. We are all people. We are all equal. We share something in common: cigars—and the hour that makes room for them. THE ROOM WE SHARE At my favorite lounge the walls are warm mustard, cream tile sits underfoot, and a drop ceiling dotted with soft lights sets the tone. Big screens glow above framed prints and old certificates; shelves run the walls with familiar bands and gadgets. Drinks live in a small room down the hall: it's BYOB, with a fridge of waters and pop and a Kcup coffee setup for anyone who wants a cup. The rule is simple—if it's in there, make yourself at home and help yourself. Rows of very comfortable leather chairs —deep-seated with supportive arms—ring low side tables for ashtrays and glasses, turning the floor into a living room. The sound of the place is conversation: a low braid of catch-ups, laughs, and the occasional play-by-play when a game matters. THE HUMIDOR (OFTEN CALLED "THE CANDY STORE") There is one humidor. It feels like stepping into a cedar library. Two long aisles run side by side, shelves pitched at an easy angle so open boxes face you like hardbacks. Track lights and a small ceiling fan push warm gold across the bands; the floor is wood, the air clean and cool. In the center sits a rolling cart—"NEW CIGARS" and Crowned Heads signs clipped to it—so you catch fresh arrivals before you even choose a wall. At the far end, a glass door looks back toward the lounge. Open, step in, close. We treat the seal like a promise; the door gives a soft woof when it's kept. Eyes first, hands second. If you handle a cigar, hold it by the band—no squeezing the leaf, no nosing the foot. Read boxes like spines, ask the host/tobacconist when you want the story behind one, and take your time. Questions are how the right stick

finds the right night. When you step out, close the door with that same soft woof so the next person walks into cedar and calm instead of air and apology. CHAIRS & THE CARD TABLE Most settle into the comfortable leather chairs—the place for quiet laughs, "how's your dad?" check-ins, and slow retrohales. Off to the side sits the card table: green felt, chip racks, friendly rivalry, and the kind of jokes that never make it to print. We float between them. Chair people wander over to kibitz between hands; table people migrate back with a fresh story and a bottle-cap trophy of a win. A few courtesies keep both lanes happy: • Leave one open seat at the table when you can—someone always wanders in mid-hand. • Keep cutters and lighters off the felt; ashtrays live at the corners. • Table volume carries excitement, not the whole room. • Rotate in after a game; nobody owns a chair. • When the deal ends, look up—names matter more than scores. CROSSING THE THRESHOLD First minutes set the night. "Welcome home," the host/tobacconist says, and you either grab a water or pop from the room down the hall, pour a quick K-cup, or set your own bottle by your chair. The humidor door woofs shut with that soft seal we love. Choose a chair by angle, not status. Lay out your cutter and lighter. Toast the foot like you're inviting the cigar to join the conversation, not trying to win it. The ember evens. Breath deepens. The house exhales. FAMILY, NOT JUST

FRIENDS This place runs on more than good air and good sticks. The friendships inside it turn into family—the kind that remembers your big day and your rough week, shows up for graduations and hospital visits, and keeps a spare chair for the person who needs it most. Most of us were new once. We got welcomed with open arms and stayed to make other people feel that same first-night relief. No cliques, no auditions. You're treated like family because that's the only way the room makes sense. A FIRST NIGHT (HOW IT STARTS) My first night began with weather. Rain chased the town into doorways, and I walked in dripping enough to apologize to the rug. "Welcome home," said the host/tobacconist, and the sentence landed like a towel across the shoulders. He pointed down the hall. "Fridge and cups that way. Help yourself." I took a water, learned the trick of the K-cup machine from a stranger who called me "brother" like we had already solved something together, and followed the cedar smell to the humidor.

Inside, I practiced the etiquette I'd overheard in five seconds: eyes first, hands by the band, questions better than guesses. I admitted I liked coffee dark and my chocolate darker, and a man with a ball cap and a calm voice pointed to a row I wouldn't have found on my own. "Medium body, a little cocoa, black pepper on the back end. Honest hour," he said. I nodded like I knew what that meant and learned later that I did. Back in the chairs, I tried to sit like I belonged without pretending that I did. The first person who spoke to me didn't ask what I did for a living. He asked what I was celebrating or surviving. It's an unfair question in the best way—too true to duck. I said I was just trying not to carry the week into tomorrow. He nodded, poured a small splash from his bottle into the glass I hadn't realized I'd carried back, and told me the cork had been waiting for a rainy night anyway. "Tiny pour," he said. "Plenty of night left." I toasted too fast. The cap-wearing man reached over with his lighter, steadying the foot and talking me through the slow circle that keeps the cherry even. "The cigar will meet you," he said. "You don't have to chase it." We watched the wrapper darken at the edges until it looked ready to keep its own pace, and something in my shoulders loosened a notch I didn't know I'd ratcheted tight. The card table behind us burst into laughter right as someone insisted he had counted correctly and someone else proved he hadn't. The joke wasn't on anyone; it was on the math. A chair got pulled out for a late arrival without ceremony. The room made room, which is how I learned you don't have to ask for permission to exist here—just for

a seat, and often not even that. By the middle third of the cigar I had learned three names, forgotten one, and been forgiven for it. Someone asked what I was smoking and, when I told him, said, "Good first pick," as if I had done something brave. I asked about the framed certificate near the TV and got the story of a long-ago tasting where the power blinked out and half the shop finished their sticks by the light of phone flashlights, people taking turns holding a beam over someone else's ash. "It's easier to smoke in the dark when the room is lit," the Librarian said, and no one needed him to explain it. A man I hadn't met yet crossed the floor with a couple of waters. "I'm headed down the hall—anyone need one next time?" he asked no one in particular and everyone at once. I said I was fine and meant it, and he nodded like that answer counted too. The talk swung to baseball, then back to work weeks, then to whether shade wrappers taste like Saturday mornings on purpose or by accident. A veteran told a quiet story in the space between innings and ash taps, and the room held still the way a room knows to when it's being trusted. When the rain slowed to drizzle, I realized I'd been there two hours without checking my phone once. I rinsed my glass, wiped the ring my bottle had left, and started to say goodnight. Two different voices said, "See you tomorrow," like it was a foregone conclusion. It was. I walked out lighter by one cigar and heavier by something I couldn't name yet. Family was the closest word, and even that one needed to sit in a chair for a while before it fit. NO AUDITIONS, NO TRIBES We don't vet people like bouncers. If you're in the room, you're in the room. A great secret of the lounge: cigars say just enough about a person to make extra questions optional. You learn what you need to know from patience, from how someone treats the humidor door, from whether they pass a cutter back with a "thank you," from the kind of joke they tell when the game goes sideways. Big topics aren't banned; people are bigger than their topics. We protect that. BYOB & HOUSE RULES (SIMPLE AND CLEAR) • BYOB. Bottles usually sit right next to their owners. Share if you want to—no labels needed. • Need a glass? They're stacked on the cabinet in the back room down the hall. Please wash, dry, and put it back before you leave. • Make yourself at home with the fridge and K-cups; leave the area tidy for the next person. •

Throw away your trash and pack out empties, or bin them the way the shop prefers. • If you make a mess—water rings, crumbs, ash—please clean it up. THE ECONOMY OF SMALL FAVORS "I'm headed down the hall—anyone need a water?" Someone says it every hour. A cutter slides across just when you reached for your pocket. A fresh ashtray appears before the old one tells your life story. You thank the person who shares a splash from their bottle without turning the moment into a lecture. Favors keep moving. When they get stuck in a speech, they stop being favors and turn into exhibits. THE LISTENING RATIO Every good room develops a listening ratio, a rhythm of talk and quiet that lets the conversation travel farther than any single story could. Try this: for every story you tell, draw two out of someone else. Ask questions that end in question marks, not apologies for your next anecdote. When they answer, repeat back a detail—"So your grandfather rolled on his porch after dinner?"—and watch the cigar they're holding become part of the story. Smoke invites honesty and cools performance. We protect that by listening like it matters. ARCHETYPES (THE FAMILY PORTRAIT) The Host–Tobacconist: one hat, same smile. Greets with "Welcome home," learns names, stitches strangers into the room, curates the humidor, watches airflow, and keeps the vibe on tempo. Points newcomers toward the self-serve drink room down the hall (BYOB) and somehow knows when to suggest a shorter stick because bedtime called ahead. They're the shop's memory and its temperature control. The Librarian: carries history without swinging it like a sword. If you ask, you get three facts, a grin, and a

recommendation that fits your night. The Coach: shows a newcomer how to cut and light, then backs off. The best Coaches make themselves obsolete in under five minutes. The Quiet Anchor: sits a little off-center, reads the room without frowning, and somehow keeps arguments from forgetting they're among friends. The Gentle Teaser: applies humor like salt—sparingly, to lift flavor, never to burn. If a joke needs a target, they make themselves the target first. The Tinkerer: loves draw tools and micro-adjustments. Handy when your burn line misbehaves, less handy with existential crises. When any of us drift into a role that crowds the room, the fix is simple: breathe, look around, and play a different part. This is family; we rotate chores. NEWCOMERS (HOW FAMILY GROWS) A newcomer is a test we grade ourselves on. The script is short and generous: "Welcome home." "First time? Want a quick tour—the humidor, chairs, drink room?" "Looking for mild, medium, or 'long week'?" "What do you like—coffee, chocolate, pepper, bread? We can match that." If she's a woman arriving solo, what changes is nothing. Same welcome, same tour, same respect, same space. If he's a young guy clutching his first purchase like he hopes the room won't notice, what changes is nothing. Same welcome, same tour, same space. The point is to let people arrive at their own speed. Push and you get performance; invite and you get presence. VENTILATION AND PEACE Air is part of hospitality. Aim your smoke away from faces; sit where the draft carries it kindly. If the door is a revolving character tonight, be the one who catches it and closes it gently. The best ventilation is a room full of people who remember that small air decisions add up to calm. RITUALS THAT BELONG TO US Welcome Home: the greeting that keeps the place soft around the edges. If you're early, say it to the next person in. If you're late, you'll hear it twice—once from the counter and once from the chairs. First Stick Fridays: bring one cigar to give away—the kind you would smoke yourself. Newcomer or old friend, someone goes home with a plan for Saturday morning and your name attached to it. Bottle Share, House Rules: small pours, many tastes, no pressure. We pass the glass like we pass a story: one turn each, then let it travel.

Water rides shotgun. Pride walks. Band Box: a wooden box on the shelf where people drop cigar bands with a date and a sentence. "Cameroon with coffee after landing that job—tasted like cinnamon and relief." The shop keeps stories; the box keeps memory. Quiet Minute at Eight: someone taps an ashtray twice. Sixty seconds of still. No speeches, no posts, no performance. Just breath. It started after a year that took too much from too many, and it stayed because it makes the next nine minutes better than the last nine.

PHONES, PHOTOS, AND PRIVACY Phones are part of life; they don't have to be part of the hour. Put yours on Do Not Disturb. If you must take a call, step out and keep it short. Photos are consent, not assumption. Ask first, always, even on event nights. Not everyone

wants their hour documented. If a photo happens, check backgrounds for people who didn't sign up to be online. A lounge is part living room, part workshop, part chapel; we guard the privacy accordingly. CHAIR

HOSTING (NO TITLE NEEDED) You don't need a badge to host. With BYOB and a self-serve fridge, hosting looks like small, steady care: when you're up, ask if anyone wants a water or pop and make a quick run; bring back extras and return empties; keep the path to the hall clear. Loan your cutter, share your light, and show newcomers where things live—the humidor, chairs, drink room, restroom—without turning it into a tour. If every regular does one small kindness per hour, the place keeps feeling like home. SEASONS OF A LOUNGE Mornings belong to readers and the self-employed—coffee cups by ashtrays, shade-wrapped sticks, conversation as quiet as the beans allow. Afternoons are errand breaks—two or three chairs occupied by people who planned an hour into their day. Evenings earn the name "crowd." Friday is a parade of jackets and denim and stories that start, "You won't believe —" When weather's kind, the patio and fire pit turn into an outdoor chapter. The rules stay; the rhythm changes.

EVENT NIGHTS WITHOUT LOSING THE ROOM

Tastings, release nights, charity raffles—crowded fun with extra variables. Show up early; take no more space than your chair. If a rep is pouring, ask one good question and listen to the answer. Don't chase seconds until everyone has firsts. If you win the raffle, act surprised even if you saw the odds. Share a taste with your neighbors. If you lose, clap anyway. Nights like this keep shops alive. They also tempt us to show off. The fix is easy: choose to leave a little good in the glass. HOW A NIGHT ENDS WELL

Endings are the proof of the ritual. If you leave in a hurry, the hour chases you; if you end on purpose, it blesses tomorrow instead of borrowing from it. Put the nub to rest while it still has a good inch left to say. Tap the ashtray; stack it with any orphans nearby. Return the borrowed lighter to its person. Wash, dry, and put away any glass you used. Pack out your empties or bin them the way the shop prefers. Wipe your spot if you left rings or crumbs. Pull the chair back under the conversation like you found it. Thank the room—quietly or out loud. Step into the night with your phone still in your pocket and let the air tell you whether you got it right. SMALL HABITS THAT CHANGE EVERYTHING Bring back two waters when you only needed one. Hold the door both directions. Learn one new name per week and use it next time. Rotate the conversation so the same three voices don't own it. Invite the person sitting alone once per month, whether they say yes or not. Show your friend how to toast slowly by doing it, not by narrating it. Stop one story early. Leave room for someone else's punchline. Say goodnight before you're tired of the people you're with. CLOSING If your shop wears different colors or keeps a different tempo, borrow the parts that fit and leave the rest—every lounge is its own good story. The social ritual isn't rules; it's muscle memory for kindness. A cigar adds fire to air and gives your hands something useful while your attention does the real work:

making room for other people to be at ease. Comfortable leather chairs, a card table, a well-kept humidor, and a self-serve fridge down the hall—BYOB and be generous. You show up, you carry your share, and somehow the room pays you back with a peace you didn't have to buy. Tomorrow morning is where you'll know whether you practiced it well. If you wake steady, not smoky—if your first thought is a name you're glad you learned and a sentence you're glad you kept to yourself—then you did it right. That's a ritual worth keeping: small, shared, and strong enough to hold an hour up to the light.

CHAPTER 8

Moderation: The Key to Unlocking Benefits

If whiskey and cigars are doors, then moderation is the key—small, ordinary, easy to overlook, and the only thing that turns the handle without breaking it. People sometimes ask for the trick, as if pleasure required a secret handshake. The trick is that there is no trick. There is the hour you choose, the pace you keep, the company you trust, and the way you end the night with enough of yourself left to greet the morning. Everything good about this lifestyle—conversation, flavor, friendship, and the steady sense that the world is big enough to hold you—hinges on that one word. Moderation unlocks the benefit; anything else borrows joy and charges interest. A QUIET CONTRACT Moderation isn't punishment. It is a contract with your future self: I'll enjoy tonight in a way that still lets you enjoy tomorrow. It is also a contract with the people in the room: I will be present, not excessive. Presence is the soul of hospitality. You can't notice the joke, or the way someone's eyes lighten when the story turns, if you have to concentrate on finding your chair. The contract is simple and specific. It starts with a question: "What am I here to do?" Celebrate? Unwind? Learn a new flavor? Catch up with a friend? Choose one. A night that tries to be all four will overspend. A night that chooses one can afford to be generous everywhere else. THE RULE OF SMALL FIRSTS There's a reason tasting rooms pour small. A small first pour and a slow first third give you time to tune your instrument. The first sips and first puffs are where you calibrate: too fast and everything flattens, too much and you'll miss the transitions. Call it the Rule of Small Firsts —start tiny, listen closely, lengthen slowly. If you still want more when the cigar hits the middle and the glass finds its voice, you're choosing with information instead of habit. THE WATER SANDWICH A simple ritual saves many nights: water–whiskey–water. Take a few sips before your first pour; approach the glass like a conversation starter, not a microphone check; then take water again before the second act. It's not about diluting pleasure. It's about reminding your palate that it has more gears than "sweet" and "strong." Water resets. Resetting lets the cigar and the whiskey keep teaching each other instead of yelling over each other. PACE IS FLAVOR Pace is the difference between taste and noise. One drink poured wide and rushed will feel louder than it is and say less than it could. One cigar puffed like a steam engine will taste like heat instead of leaf. Most people discover the same truth the first time they slow down: flavor returns in layers—bread before honey, cedar before cocoa, pepper that moves from tongue to nose and back again with the retrohale. Moderation is not half the fun. It is where fun becomes detail. THE CHECKPOINTS THAT KEEP YOU HONEST Because honesty is easier to keep than to recover, build a few checkpoints into your hour: • The Nose Test: Before the first sip, nose the glass and name two notes out loud, even if you're alone. If you can't name them, the pour is too big or you're moving too fast. • The Middle-Third Question: Halfway through the cigar, ask: "Am I still tasting or just smoking?" If the answer is "just smoking," put it down for two minutes. Let the ember cool. You'll be surprised what comes back. • The Friend Test: Could you repeat what your friend just said, more or less word for word? If not, you're in the wrong lane. • The Walkaway Rule: If you can't walk to the counter and back without thinking about it, the night is over. Not punished—over. Ending well is how the next night begins well.

THE HUMOR OF MODERATION Moderation has a sense of humor. It's the line that makes a table laugh without needing to make a second one to prove it wasn't an accident. It's the confidence to leave a drink unfinished because the conversation finished first. The people who seem most at ease in a lounge are rarely the ones trying to set records. They are the ones practicing a small, almost invisible courage: the courage to stop while the hour is still singing. THE DIFFERENCE BETWEEN RULES AND RITUALS Rules tell you what not to do; rituals remind you what you're doing. We need a few of both. A rule might be "never drive after drinking." That's not moderation—that's morality. A ritual might be "pour with your non-dominant hand." It slows you down just enough to remember that the glass carries a story, not a dare. Another ritual: set your phone to Do Not Disturb before the first light. Anything that can wait an hour will be gentler when you get to it. Anything that can't wait deserves a sober head. THE TWO-GLASS MYTH Moderation has enemies, and myths are the craftiest. One says, "Two glasses is always moderate." Another says, "I can make up for tonight by being extra-good tomorrow." Both miss the point. The body doesn't use a ledger. It uses moments. If the moment asks for slow attention, pouring a second to meet a number is nonsense. If the moment asks you to stop, but you keep going because you've decided on a quota, that's also nonsense.

Moderation listens. It does not negotiate with math after midnight. FOOD IS A FRIEND, EXCUSES ARE NOT A meal steadies the ship. A bite of bread can quiet a palate that's gotten too spicy; a handful of nuts can give a second wind to someone who went too long between lunch and lounge. But "I ate a lot, so I can drink a lot" is a shortcut to the worst version of yourself. Food helps; it doesn't absolve. Use it like ballast, not like a shield. THE LAST POUR RULE If the table is laughing and the ash is stacking neatly and someone reaches for the bottle at the exact moment you think, "This has been a good night," you are standing at the border between "good" and "too much." The Last Pour Rule is simple: when you have the thought, count to twenty, take a sip of water, and ask, "What would make the next ten minutes great?" If your answer involves a second pour, pour half as much as you thought. If your answer involves telling a story you've already told once, skip both the pour and the story. Leave a little good in the glass and in the room. THE OFF SWITCH Moderation is possible only if you can find your off switch. Everyone's is different. For some it is a curfew—"I'm out at nine, no matter what." For others it is a fixed number of puffs or a rule about proof—"Nothing over this line on weeknights." Some choose "one cigar or one drink, never both, unless I'm home for the night." Whatever you choose, make it public to yourself. Say it out loud when you arrive. The room will help you keep it. The best lounges are full of people who believe in each other's tomorrows. A WORD ABOUT STRENGTH Strength is not the same as body. Body is the weight of flavor. Strength is the weight of consequences. A full-bodied whiskey at a modest proof can be a velvet voice; a light-bodied whiskey at a high proof can sneak up on you like a bad idea wearing a good suit. The same goes for cigars: a light wrapper doesn't always mean a light touch. Part of moderation is reading labels and your own history: what hits you fast, what lingers longer than you like, what pairs well with conversation and what asks for a quieter chair than tonight offers. A WEEK BUILT FOR TOMORROW The easiest way to moderate is to treat your week like a garden. You don't water every day; you water when it matters, and you let the soil rest. Pick two nights where you savor and three or four where you don't. The math can

shift with seasons, work, and family, but the principle holds. Rest makes flavor louder. If you doubt it, take a week off, then light a favorite on Friday. The first sip and first inch will feel like the volume knob discovered new numbers. THE GRACE TO SAY NO There will be nights when you don't want a pour at all and someone offers you one like a gift wrapped in insistence. Practice this sentence: "I'm good, but I'd love to smell what you're having." It honors the offer without surrendering your plan. Most people respect that. If they don't, you've identified the person you should sit further from next week. THE

GENTLE ART OF SHARING If you pour for someone else, pour small. Let them ask for more. The best hosts live by a principle you can write on the side of a Glencairn: Never pour a second before the first is mostly a story. If the glass is still full when the story ends, your pour was too big or the night too busy. Either way, the solution isn't to pour again; it's to let the conversation stand on its own two feet. MISTAKES HAPPEN No one gets moderation perfect. You will overshoot sometimes. The important thing is what happens next. Apologize quickly if you got louder than you needed to be. Drink water before sleep. Leave the car where it is and ride home with a friend or a service. Let the mistake make you kinder to the next person who's learning the same lesson. We remember mercy longer than we remember lectures. THE TECH THAT HELPS (AND WHEN TO IGNORE IT) Watches can count steps, breaths, and sometimes even how restless you were after midnight. If a gadget helps you notice that you sleep better on nights you kept the key, keep the gadget. But don't outsource judgment. A device can't taste for you, won't notice whether you listened, and is no use against peer pressure that dresses up as camaraderie. Moderation is an inside job helped by outside reminders. THE COMPANY YOU KEEP Rooms teach moderation. Sit near people who pour with care and laugh with ease and say goodnight while the chairs still feel warm. The best mentoring is side-channel: not a speech, just a pattern that repeats until it becomes yours. The quickest way to forget your plan is to park next to the table that prides itself on excess. You don't have to dislike them. You just have to love tomorrow more than you love their applause. A FEW PRACTICES THAT NEVER FAIL • Half-Size Glass, Full-Sized Night: A smaller glass makes smaller pours feel natural. It is not a trick; it is a design choice. • Set the First End Time: Decide when you will leave before you arrive, then tell one person you trust. The commitment will do the rest. • Alternate

Proof: Follow a higher-proof pour with a lower-proof or a mocktail. Your palate will thank you; your stories will continue to make sense. • Savor, Don't Stockpile: If you're collecting bottles instead of moments, moderation will feel like deprivation. If you're collecting moments, moderation will feel like style. WHAT MODERATION IS NOT Moderation is not performative suffering. It does not need an audience. It does not make you better than the person next to you; it makes you better for them. It does not count other people's glasses or police their ash. If a friend asks for help, give it. If they don't, give them room. Our job is to make the hour safe for everyone who chose to share it. THE MIDNIGHT TEST Right before you leave, take a breath and run the Midnight Test:

1) Can you clearly name three flavors from the glass and two from the cigar?

2) Can you recall the best moment of the night in one sentence?

3) Is there enough of you left to text a kind word to someone who wasn't there? If you can do all three without effort, you kept the key. If you can't, that's all right. Keys get lost. Tomorrow you'll find it again on the hook by the door where you meant to leave it all along. HOW THE LOUNGE HELPS Good rooms make moderation easier without calling attention to it. They keep water handy. They offer small cups for people who want to taste and bigger ones for those who know what they're doing. They do not make jokes about saying no. They cheer good endings. They treat the ride home like part of hospitality: if anyone's in doubt, someone says, "I'll drive." A room like that teaches you to want tomorrow as much as you want tonight. SCRIPTS THAT SAVE YOU Sometimes you need a sentence ready to go: • "I'm pacing this one." (Translation: I'm enjoying this; please stop trying to

improve it.) • "I'm driving." (The conversation ends here if people are decent.) • "Pour me half and I'll come back to it." (You probably won't. That's the point.) • "This is my last light." (Say it out loud, and you'll keep it.) • "I'm good with water." (Said confidently, it sounds like a choice instead of a loss.) These aren't apologies. They are boundaries spoken kindly. Good friends will help you hold them. HOLIDAY & BIG-EVENT GAME PLAN December parties, Super Bowl spreads, birthdays, release nights—occasions stretch the edges of moderation. Use a plan that survives noise:

4) Name Your Job. Decide your role before you arrive: driver, host, taster, storyteller, photographer. Jobs are guardrails.

5) Plate Before Pour. Eat first. Bread, protein, something green. Your palate and your pace will both improve.

6) Proof Ladder. Start low, climb one rung if the night asks, climb back down before you leave.

7) Water Buddy. Keep a water within reach of the glass; every time you touch one, touch the other.

8) Small Glass, Big Cheers. Bring your own smaller glass if you must; nobody argues with a person who came prepared.

9) One Share, Not Three. If you brought a special bottle, pour tiny tastes for a few people you want to remember sharing it with—then put the cork back in. Scarcity protects memory.

10) Call Your Last Light Early. If midnight is the target, make your last light at ten. Let the last inch be conversation, not negotiation.

11) Exit Line Ready. "I want to remember this exactly as it is." Works every time and feels like a toast, not a retreat.

12) Keys Sorted First. Before the first pour, know exactly how you're getting home. If the plan changes, the night changes with it: water only.

13) Next-Day Ritual. Coffee, walk, text the host thanks. Moderation pays dividends when you collect them.

FIELD NOTES: OBSERVATIONS FROM MANY LOUNGES The following are practical observations gathered over years of nights that went right and a few that didn't. No fiction, just patterns: • Early arrivals moderate better. People who show up before the room peaks find a pace that's hard to match if you drop into the middle of a roar. • Water within reach is everything. If you can stretch a hand and touch water without looking, you'll drink it; if you have to stand, you won't. • Small kindnesses lower pressure. When regulars offer a lift unprompted or keep an extra bottle of club soda in the fridge, moderation becomes normal instead of heroic.

• The humidor teaches patience. People who browse slowly also sip slowly. Making one careful choice there often leads to better choices in the glass. • Chairs talk. Closer to the TV equals faster pours; closer to the door equals earlier goodbyes. Seat choice is a strategy. • Newcomers copy the first person who welcomed them. If that person sets a pace, the newcomer will match it. If that person treats excess like a joke, so will the newcomer. • Weeks with two planned nights beat weeks with four "we'll see" nights. Unplanned pleasure turns into reflex; planned pleasure turns into ritual. • Generosity works best in teaspoons. Passing tastes beats pushing refills. "Try a sip" is moderation's best friend. • Cleanup makes endings real. Washing a glass and resetting a side table is the body's way of telling the brain the night is complete. A PRACTICAL TOOLKIT Pack light; these few items cover most nights:

— A smaller glass or Glencairn. — A refillable water bottle. — Breath mints or gum (for the ride home, not during the cigar). — A pen or notes app template titled "Tonight's Notes" with slots for glass flavor, cigar flavor, best moment, and exit time. — A rideshare app logged in with payment ready. — Cash for snacks and tipping the person who kept the room steady. DECISION TREE (TEXT VERSION) Before the first pour, walk this tree: • Driving home? → Water only. If your plan changes, your night changes with it. • Not driving? → Do you have an end time? — Yes → Set an alarm for ten minutes before it. — No → Choose one now and tell a friend. • Are you pairing? — Yes → Pour small, taste, then adjust to the cigar. — No → Keep the glass modest and let the cigar lead. • Feeling stressed? — Yes → Start with water for five minutes. Pleasure needs room. — No → Proceed with the Rule of Small Firsts. SELF-CHECKS DURING THE NIGHT Quarter-time: Can you remember your first impression of the glass and the cigar without looking at notes? Halftime: Are you sipping water every couple of minutes? Is the ash even? Three-quarter-time: Can you name one person's story from tonight? Final whistle: Can you leave ten minutes earlier than planned and feel satisfied? Try it once. See what changes. POST-NIGHT RESET Moderation gets easier when the morning rewards you: • Hydrate again. • Light breakfast with protein and something bright (citrus or apple). • Ten-minute walk outside. • Review "Tonight's Notes" and circle one decision you're proud of. Write one sentence about what you'll repeat next time. COMMON TRAPS & HOW TO STEP AROUND THEM Trap: The refill you didn't notice.

Fix: Keep the bottle out of reach; make refills a deliberate walk. Trap: Social momentum. Fix: Excuse yourself for a water run. Physical movement breaks momentum without drama. Trap: "Just one more" when the story ended. Fix: Ask a question instead of pouring: "What was your favorite part of tonight?" Trap: Proof creep—bottles climb as the night does. Fix: Pick a ceiling before you start; tell one person. Trap: Hunger masquerading as thirst. Fix: Snack early—nuts, crackers, a sandwich—so you're choosing flavor, not calories. CHECKLISTS YOU CAN SCREENSHOT Arrival: water, phone on Do Not Disturb, end time set, ride plan clear. Midnight Test: three flavors from glass, two from cigar, one-sentence memory. Exit: glass rinsed, spot clean, thanks given, keys to a safe driver or left in pocket while you wait for your ride.

RESPECTFUL HOSTING IN A BYOB LOUNGE Hosting without bartending looks like this: • Point newcomers to the drink room down the hall and the K-cups. • Offer small tastes from your bottle when asked, never uninvited refills. • Keep shared snacks where everyone can reach them; label anything you brought for a friend and keep it with you. • Model moderation by leaving on time and cleaning your spot. • Thank the host/tobacconist; they set the tone you're benefiting from. THE LONG GAME Moderation is not about tonight; it's about years. The pleasure you can keep repeating without regret is the only pleasure worth practicing. The goal isn't to be remembered as the person who could keep going. The goal is to be remembered as the person who kept coming back, steady and kind, able to listen and laugh, to teach a new hand a simple cut and to stay long enough to hear what people mean when they say they had a week. YOUR PERSONAL POLICY Write one page called My Policy. It has three lines: 1) Why I enjoy this (people, flavor, a quiet hour). 2) How I protect it (pace, water, small pours, off nights). 3) Where I stop (a curfew, a limit, a ride plan). Keep it in your wallet or your notes app. Read it once a month. Policies are not romantic, but neither are broken plans. The point is not to impress anyone. The point is to remember who you said you were when you weren't being tempted to be someone else. THE BENEFIT YOU CAN FEEL The benefits of this lifestyle aren't mystical. They are simple and sturdy: conversations that go somewhere, sleep that actually rests you, mornings that start clear, friendships that grow because the people in them show up the same way next time. Moderation doesn't guarantee any of that, but it makes all of it possible. The longer you practice, the more you'll notice that the best nights feel almost identical: honest pour, honest leaf, honest goodbye. A BENEDICTION FOR THE WALK TO THE CAR Stand, stretch, rinse the glass if you used one, return the lighter that isn't yours, take a last look around the room to

see if anyone needs a hand, and then step into the night. If the sky is clear, notice it. If it's raining, wear it like weather, not a metaphor. Tell yourself one true sentence —"I kept the key tonight"—and then prove it by keeping it again tomorrow.

CHAPTER 9

Myths, Misconceptions, and the Anti-Cigar Crusade

The loudest ideas about cigars rarely come from people who smoke them. That's not a complaint; it's an observation from years spent around cedar and conversation. Sound bites travel faster than nuance, and in the rush, myths multiply: that every cigar is a cigarette in disguise, that a single puff rewrites your future, that a lounge is a recruiting office, that the only reasons to enjoy a cigar are ignorance or denial. This chapter is not a fight. It's a clarification. We will name the common myths, explain why they stick, and offer plain practices that keep the culture adult, courteous, and honest. Two promises first. One: we will not wave away risk. Combustion is not kale. Smoke is real. Nicotine is real. Adults make adult choices, and those choices deserve sober respect. Two: we will not exaggerate. Exaggeration invites eye rolls and turns honest conversation into a contest. The point here isn't victory. It's clarity. WHAT A MYTH IS AND WHY IT STICKS A myth is a shortcut—a story that travels light, repeats easily, and sounds helpful even when it is only half true. Myths stick for three reasons: • They simplify fear. "All smoke is the same" is easier to say than "Patterns of use differ." • They scale. Broad rules are easier to enforce than precise ones, even when precision would be fairer. • They reward outrage. Social media prefers heat over light; a post that scolds will outpace a paragraph that explains. The antidote is not a counter-myth. It is patient detail, offered with a tone that refuses to become what it opposes. MYTH #1: "A CIGAR IS JUST A CIGARETTE IN A TUXEDO."

Reality: Premium cigars and factory-made cigarettes differ in leaf, construction, additives, culture, and typical patterns of use. Cigarettes are engineered for quick, frequent inhalation; premium cigars are whole-leaf products designed to be savored slowly, commonly without inhalation, often in adult-only social settings. The difference does not make cigars "safe." It makes them different—especially in pace, frequency, and expectations.

Why the myth persists: from a distance, all smoke looks like smoke. Regulation often prefers one category called "tobacco" because nuance is administratively cheaper. That convenience blurs meaningful distinctions. Practical takeaway: talk about patterns. Frequency, inhalation, and setting matter. Honest comparisons acknowledge both overlap and difference without pretending that difference cancels risk. MYTH #2: "ONE CIGAR IS A MEDICAL EVENT." Reality: The human body is resilient and complicated. Risk lives in patterns. The lifestyle described in this book emphasizes moderation, adult spaces, and a pace that prioritizes presence over consumption. That approach does not erase risk; it locates risk where it belongs: in accumulated habits, not singular moments staged for a headline. Why the myth persists: dramatic claims get attention. "This specific behavior in this dose, in this context, over this span, carries these tradeoffs" does not fit on a billboard. Practical takeaway: decline absolutist language. Replace "never/always" with "more/less." Replace "proof" with "context." Choose behaviors you can defend in daylight. MYTH #3: "NICOTINE MEANS INEVITABLE ADDICTION." Reality: Nicotine can produce dependence; pretending otherwise insults adult readers. But dependence is influenced

by dose, route, frequency, and intention. People who enjoy premium cigars occasionally, without inhalation, and within a community that prizes conversation over compulsion, report a very different experience than people using products engineered for repeated, rapid hits. Different does not mean harmless; it means the likelihood and shape of dependence vary with behavior. Why the myth persists: fear prefers certainty. "Inevitable" is tidy. "It depends on pattern and person" requires thought. Practical takeaway: keep a personal policy. Decide when and how often you partake; write it down; stick to it. Independence is easier to protect than to recover. MYTH #4: "SECONDHAND

SMOKE MAKES ALL LOUNGES IRRESPONSIBLE."

Reality: Courtesy and ventilation are central to adult spaces. Well-run lounges control airflow, mind their neighbors, and take pride in being good citizens. Even so, smoke is smoke; the respectful position isn't to argue that everyone must love what you love. It is to keep smoke where smoke belongs: in designated, adult spaces with people who choose to be there. Why the myth persists: bad actors make better footage. A careless patio can write a script for an entire city. Practical takeaway: be a better neighbor than the ordinance requires. Doors closed, patios mindful, late-night voices low, sidewalks clean. Courtesy is advocacy with a broom in its hand. MYTH #5: "CIGAR CULTURE TARGETS KIDS." Reality: Premium cigar shops are adult businesses. They depend on long-term relationships with adults who value service and community. The vibe is couches and conversation, not candy displays. If a shop behaves otherwise, customers should walk and explain why. Why the myth persists: "protecting kids" is the one argument that rarely gets challenged, even when applied sloppily. It's also easy to confuse bright packaging with intent. A colorful box does not equal kid marketing. Practical takeaway: support strict ID policies; applaud shops that enforce them; shut down any joke that blurs the line. Adult culture is safest when it is obviously adult. MYTH #6: "IF YOU ENJOY CIGARS, YOU MUST DENY SCIENCE." Reality: Respecting science means reading it carefully. Studies vary in quality, methodology, and relevance to premium cigar use. Many aggregate all tobacco or focus on cigarette populations, then slide the conclusions across the table to cover every product and pattern. Reasonable questions include: Who was studied? How often? Inhale or not? What else was happening— alcohol, environment, work stress? None of those questions "beat science." They are science. Why the myth persists: headlines condense; nuance bleeds. The phrase "linked to" does a lot of heavy lifting without distinguishing correlation from cause. Practical takeaway: when a scary headline appears, run a quick checklist—what product and pattern were studied; relative vs absolute numbers; confounders; and how cautious the authors actually were. Uncertainty is not denial. It's honesty. MYTH #7: "PAIRING WHISKEY AND CIGARS DOUBLES THE DAMAGE." Reality: Harm does not stack like Lego bricks. Alcohol and tobacco each carry risks shaped by dose and habit. Pairing does not automatically double anything; excess does. The practical distinction is moderation: small pours, slow cadence, water within reach, and nights planned for conversation rather than collection. Why the myth persists: compound warnings sound persuasive even when they ignore behavior. Practical takeaway: practice what Chapter 8 outlined—pace, water, end time, and a plan for the ride home. Pair flavor, not volume. MYTH #8: "ALL SMOKE IS THE SAME, SO ALL POLICIES SHOULD BE THE SAME." Reality: Policy lives at the intersection of fairness and practicality. It's fair to distinguish premium cigars from massmarket products on the basis of leaf, additives, and typical use; it's practical to enforce rules that reflect how real people behave. One-size-fits-all bans satisfy simplicity at the cost of sense. Why the myth persists: administrators prefer uniform categories. Uniform categories prefer uniform penalties. Practical takeaway: when you speak to policymakers, be specific without being combative. Use nouns, not adjectives: "whole-leaf," "non-inhalation," "adult-only lounges," "occasional use." Offer measurable commitments: ventilation standards, posted rules, ID compliance, exterior cleanup. Complaints without proposals sound like noise. Proposals sound like citizenship. MYTH #9: "CIGAR LEAF IS CHEMICAL HEAVY." Reality: Premium cigars are built from fermented, whole tobacco leaf, typically without the flavor additives and paper seen in other products. Fermentation is a biological process—heat, time, and pressure—that tames harshness and develops aroma. But we should be adults about this: combustion still produces byproducts. "Natural" is not a shield. The honest position is that craftsmanship and care can elevate the experience but not absolve it. Why the myth persists: people love the word "chemical." Everything is chemical—even water—but the word has become a scarecrow that doesn't require argument. Practical takeaway: skip talisman words. Instead of "pure" or "chemical-free," use "whole leaf," "fermented," and "well-constructed." Plain words, true meanings. MYTH #10: "THE LOUNGE IS A RECRUITMENT CENTER." Reality: A well-run lounge is more like a library with laughter. It's a place where adults who already enjoy cigars come to slow down and talk. Newcomers are typically adults who arrive by choice, not through marketing campaigns. The culture encourages learning etiquette and choosing carefully, not collecting converts. Why the myth persists: any group that enjoys something together can look like it's recruiting. Sometimes enthusiasts get enthusiastic. Practical takeaway: model consent in conversation. If someone shows interest, answer questions. If someone doesn't, let the hour speak for itself. MYTH #11: "IF YOU LIKE THE SMELL, YOU'RE IGNORING THE HAZARD." Reality: Preference and risk are separate. Liking the aroma doesn't sanitize chemistry; disliking it doesn't prove harm. Civility keeps them distinct: acknowledge that aroma is part of the appeal and keep smoke in adult spaces with voluntary participation. Why the myth persists: arguments confuse taste with safety because taste is immediate while safety is statistical. Practical takeaway: lead with boundaries, not opinions. "We keep smoke here, with consent" ends more debates than "But it smells good." MYTH #12: "CIGAR PEOPLE

ARE JUSTIFYING A BAD HABIT." Reality: People who take cigars seriously spend more time discussing how to behave than how to excuse themselves. They write house rules, plan rides, clean up after themselves, and keep an eye on newcomers. That's not justification; that's stewardship. You can disagree with the activity and still recognize the ethic. Why the myth persists: the worst examples in any group become surrogates for the whole.

Practical takeaway: keep the ethic visible—trash where it belongs, glassware rinsed, goodbyes timely, kindness routine. Behavior is the only rebuttal that doesn't require a speech. MYTH #13: "CIGAR SMOKE LINGERS FOREVER AND RUINS BUILDINGS." Reality: Odor management is part of operating responsibly, and modern lounges invest in airflow, filtration, and cleaning routines. Soft surfaces and poor ventilation trap aroma; hard surfaces and steady airflow release it. Buildings aren't ruined by presence; they are disrespected by neglect. Why the myth persists: the worst maintained rooms become the example everyone remembers. Practical takeaway: ventilation on, doors closed, filters changed, surfaces wiped, jackets that can carry aroma kept separate. Cleanliness is policy you can smell. MYTH #14: "CIGAR SHOPS ARE BOYS' CLUBS." Reality: Many lounges are deliberately inclusive —women, couples, younger and older adults, newcomers, veterans. The currency is manners, not demographics. The best rooms shut down gatekeeping fast. Why the myth persists: a few loud rooms earn reputations that outlive them. Practical takeaway: make inclusion explicit. Greet everyone the same. No jokes that hinge on who belongs. Mixed company makes better conversation and better policy. MYTH #15: "PRICE EQUALS QUALITY, AND CULTURE EQUALS ELITISM." Reality: Price reflects scarcity, marketing, construction, leaf, and overhead—not simply flavor. There are great, honest sticks at working-person prices and disappointing rarities with fancy bands.

The lifestyle described here is blue-collar at heart: bring what you enjoy, share what you can, treat everyone's selection with respect. Why the myth persists: luxury imagery is louder than ordinary good sense. Practical takeaway: separate taste from status. Recommend experiences, not price points. The best compliment is "that fits your night," not "that proves something." MYTH #16: "EVENT NIGHTS ARE EXCUSES TO OVERDRINK." Reality: Release nights and tastings survive because the community behaves. Good shops set expectations—water on hand, modest pours, bottle sharing handled with a light touch, rides sorted before corks move. Everyone goes home safe, which is the only victory that matters. Why the myth persists: a single messy story travels farther than a hundred quiet successes. Practical takeaway: host like you mean it —small cups, visible water, clear close time, and a culture that applauds early goodbyes. HOW TO READ A SCARY HEADLINE (A SIMPLE GUIDE) Before forwarding an

article that claims shocking risk, try this five-step approach:
1) Population: Was the study about premium cigar users,
cigarette users, or "tobacco users" as a combined category?
2) Pattern: Daily, occasional, non-inhalation? If the paper
doesn't say, be careful about the leap from "tobacco" to
"cigars." 3) Outcome: What was actually measured—
diagnoses, biomarkers, self-reported symptoms,
hospitalizations? 4) Numbers: Relative risk ("40%
increase") can sound large while absolute numbers are
small. Look for context. 5) Confounders: Were alcohol use,
diet, stress, or workplace exposures considered? You don't
need a PhD to ask those questions. You need patience.
Asking them out loud in the lounge improves everyone's
literacy.

ARGUING LESS, EXPLAINING BETTER One of
the kindest strategies in public is to stop trying to "win"
and start trying to inform. Phrases that serve clarity: • "I
can only speak to premium cigars and adult lounges; that's

the culture I know." • "Risk isn't zero, but pattern matters. Occasional, non-inhalation use in adult spaces is a different pattern than daily inhalation." • "We support strict ID policies and good ventilation. Courtesy is part of the culture." • "If this isn't for you, I respect that. We keep it in its lane." Each sentence avoids provocations and invites a more productive conversation. If the other party prefers provocation, consider spending your hour elsewhere.

ETIQUETTE AS ADVOCACY Etiquette isn't decoration. It's the daily work that keeps privileges from turning into problems. In practice that means: • Boundaries: smoke only where invited; ask before lighting on patios or at events. • Neighbors: acknowledge nearby businesses; manage parking and noise; sweep sidewalks before you leave. • Clothes & Courtesy: carry a jacket that can hold aroma without lending it to every chair; ask before hugging someone who didn't share the hour. • Consent for Photos: never post images of people in a lounge without explicit permission. Privacy outlasts your feed. Every small act communicates, "We are careful with what we love."

DIFFERENCES THAT REALLY DO MATTER

Advocates sometimes overstate difference; critics sometimes erase it. Hold the center by naming factors that change the conversation: • Leaf and Construction: whole-leaf, hand-rolled products behave differently than reconstituted ones. • Use Pattern: occasional vs daily; social setting vs solitary breaks; non-inhalation vs inhalation. • Duration: an hour with one cigar has a different rhythm than ten short breaks with something engineered for speed. • Community: a moderated, adult community regulates itself; it praises good endings and rides home. None of this claims immunity. It claims context. DATA LITERACY MINI-GLOSSARY (FOR CIVIL DISCUSSIONS) • Association: two things travel together; may not cause each other. • Causation: changing one reliably changes the other, all else equal. • Relative Risk: comparison between groups (sounds big). • Absolute Risk: the baseline numbers (keeps scale honest). • Confidence Interval: range that contains the true effect with a stated probability (wide = uncertain). • Confounder: a third factor that can explain part of the observed effect. When someone throws numbers, these terms let you ask useful questions without turning the conversation into a duel. A CHECKLIST FOR ETHICAL CIGAR SHOPS (SELF-AUDIT) 1) Verified 21+ entry with ID. 2) Posted house rules—ventilation, BYOB expectations, cleanup, photography consent. 3) Water visible and free; non-alcohol options easy. 4) Ventilation maintained; filters changed on schedule. 5) Neighbors' concerns logged and addressed within a week.

6) Sidewalk and entry cleaned nightly.

7) Staff trained to decline sales politely if someone appears impaired.

8) Inclusivity isn't a sign; it's behavior—welcome everyone, shut down gatekeeping.

9) Events capped by time, not by how much is left in a bottle.

10) Rides encouraged; staff comfortable calling a ride for customers.

11) Humidor etiquette taught kindly to newcomers.

12) Social media: celebrate community, never shame anyone, never post without consent. Shops that live this list rarely face hostility for long; neighbors notice steadiness. SPEAKING TO FAMILY WHO DON'T SHARE THE HOBBY You can love your people and your pastime without making either feel second. A few scripts: • "I change clothes after the lounge so I don't bring the aroma into the house." • "I plan two nights a week and keep the others free." • "If we have plans early, I skip the night before." • "I enjoy the company as much as the cigar; happy to meet you for dinner first." Respect prevents resentment. Your family may never adore cigars.

They don't have to adore them to accept that you carry yourself responsibly. WHEN "CRUSADE" SHOWS UP Some campaigns against cigars are animated by genuine concern; others by platforms looking for content. Either way, learn to recognize patterns: • Guilt by Association: citing statistics about cigarettes to regulate cigars. • Motivation Minimizing: assuming any defense of nuance is just self-interest. • The Slippery Slope: "If we make one exception, everything collapses." • Moral Crowding: turning personal boundaries into universal mandates. The answer is not reciprocal sarcasm. Keep describing how the culture actually operates: adult-only spaces, moderation, consent, stewardship. If you repeat those pillars calmly, you'll outlast the heat. POLICY: SPEAKING LIKE A CITIZEN If you care enough to write or speak in public, do it well. Keep your message crisp: •

Acknowledge risk. People listen longer when you're not minimizing reality. • Describe the product. Whole-leaf, hand-rolled, adult-use, occasional patterns. • Offer commitments. ID checks, ventilation, posted rules, cleanup. • Ask for proportion. Distinct rules for distinct products and patterns. • Be local. Cite how your shop behaves; name owners and contributions to the neighborhood. No slogans, no threats. Adults, speaking to adults, about adult spaces. TEN SHORT REFRAINS FOR CIVIL CONVERSATIONS

13) "Different isn't 'safe,' but it's still different."

14) "We keep our hobby where it belongs."

15) "Courtesy prevents more problems than arguments ever solve."

16) "Frequency matters; inhalation matters; context matters."

17) "I don't need everyone to agree; I need us to coexist."

18) "We're strict about ID because we care about being here next year."

19) "If this isn't for you, thanks for letting it be for me —over there."

20) "Small pours, slow puffs, early goodbyes."

21) "Clean sidewalks convince more neighbors than Facebook posts."

22) "The room is better when we act like we'll see each other tomorrow."

COMMON MISCONCEPTIONS INSIDE THE CULTURE (YES, OURS) Let's be fair: myths aren't only external. We have a few to retire. • "I can handle anything." Maybe—but why? Restraint is a better story than endurance. • "Strong equals good." Strength is one axis; balance and flavor are others. • "Newer is always better." Hype has a half-life. Keep a core of dependable sticks you actually enjoy. • "If I'm generous, I have to over-pour." No. Generosity is attention, not volume. • "We're above criticism because we're nice." Courtesy earns patience, not exemption. Keep listening. CASE STUDIES WITHOUT DRAMA (REAL PATTERNS, NO NAMES) • The Courteous Patio: A shop adds wind screens and limits outdoor hours; nearby businesses change from annoyed to supportive. Cleanup at close becomes ritual. • The Early Goodbye: A group sets a weeknight rule to end by ten. Attendance holds; mornings improve. • The Water Stack: A fridge down the hall gets stocked with water and club soda. Pour sizes drop by half without anyone writing a memo. • The ID Moment: A regular forgets his wallet and gets turned away kindly. Everyone notices that rules aren't theater. These are small, boring wins—the kind the outside world rarely sees. Boring wins keep rooms open. THE PHILOSOPHY UNDER THE PRACTICE This book returns to the same center: agency with humility. You choose your habits; you carry their weight; you behave like your choices share space with other humans who did not audition for your movie. Agency without humility becomes entitlement. Humility without agency becomes fear. Together they become culture, which is stronger than any single argument about preference. CLOSING: NUANCE ISN'T A LOOPHOLE People sometimes hear nuance as a lawyer's trick. It isn't. Nuance is what grownups owe each other when the world is complicated and shared. You can defend adult spaces without denying risk. You can love flavor without mocking caution. You can hold a cigar in one hand and responsibility in the other, and you can do it in a way that makes the room better for everyone in it and outside it. If the loudest story about cigars is still a caricature after this chapter, that's all right. Caricatures thrive on distance. Real life is close-up: a well-kept humidor; an hour protected by manners; water within reach; ID at the counter; a sidewalk swept; an early goodnight; a morning that begins clear. This is the counter-

narrative that needs no exclamation points. It just needs

repetition—quiet, steady, and true.

CHAPTER 10

Whiskey's Hidden Health Contributions

Let's put the cards on the table up front. Whiskey is not medicine, not a multivitamin, and not a permission slip. It is a crafted spirit that can play a positive role in a well-lived life when it stays small, slow, and social. This chapter is about those subtle contributions—the "hidden" ways the whiskey ritual can support well-being for some adults—without pretending that a bottle is a doctor. We'll talk about what moderation looks like in the real world, how the sensory ritual can lower stress, how community sharpens the mind and lifts the mood, and how to structure your week so that enjoyment doesn't borrow against tomorrow. When we use a word like "benefit," we're talking about lived experience and common-sense practice, not clinical promises. If you have any reason to avoid alcohol—medical, personal, spiritual—skip the pour and keep the ritual. Most of the good in this chapter survives perfectly with a glass of water or tea. WHAT "MODERATION" MEANS IN PRACTICE

You've seen tasting rooms do it right. Small pours, big attention, water always within reach. Translating that into everyday life: • Start with a tasting pour, not a "drink." Think in ounces the way a chef thinks in pinches. A neat or Glencairn pour of around an ounce—give or take—is more than enough for real flavor exploration. • Keep proof in mind. High-proof whiskey asks for smaller measures and slower pacing—dilute with a few drops of water if the nose feels hot. • Pair whiskey with time, not with volume. Give yourself a fixed window and let the glass live inside it; don't let the glass expand the night. • Build in dry days. Pleasure that has places to rest comes back stronger. • Never drive after drinking, period. No exceptions. Your ride plan is part of the ritual. RITUAL, NOT RUSH: HOW THE PROCESS CALMS THE BODY A surprising amount of the "good" that people feel from whiskey has nothing to do with ethanol. It comes from ritual—slowly repeated steps that cue the nervous system to downshift. Consider the simple sequence below and notice that none of it requires a pour: 1) Set the space. Sit, place a glass, arrange light, put your phone on Do Not Disturb. 2) Breathe before you begin. Four in, hold four, six out. Two rounds. 3) Nose the empty glass. The faint oak, the memory of previous pours—this is a cue to pay attention, not to hurry. 4) Pour small and still. Watch the legs, not because they tell you everything, but because watching something settle teaches you to settle. 5) Nose, sip, note. Name two aromas, one flavor, one texture. You're giving your brain a short, focused task. Focus is the opposite of fuss. Those quiet mechanics matter. Slowing breath nudges the parasympathetic system. Naming aromas recruits language centers that prefer calm over chaos. Tiny behavior changes cascade; many people feel physically different after two minutes of ritual even if they never take a sip. THE SOCIAL LIFT: WHY COMPANY CHANGES THE EXPERIENCE The old definition of health includes social well-being, not just the absence of illness. A good lounge or home circle functions as a third place—neither work nor home—where the conversation is the point and the bottle is background. That matters. Laughing with people who know your week takes weight off your shoulders in ways solitary scrolling never will. Listening does more than distract; it organizes your thoughts so tomorrow feels navigable. A whiskey night done right is basically a peer-led decompression chamber. Practical ways to increase the social lift: • Sit where people talk more than they watch a screen. • Ask real questions and let answers breathe. • Bring something you're curious about rather than something you want people to praise. Curiosity invites curiosity. • Share small tastes, not big refills. Generosity measured in teaspoons keeps minds clear and conversations generous. SENSORY TRAINING: A WORKOUT FOR ATTENTION AND MEMORY Nosing and tasting are attention sports. You sort signals (grain, oak, spice), recall memories (vanilla like your grandmother's kitchen, orange zest like that holiday dessert), and try to name them. That little workout bridges attention, memory, and language— the very skills that get dulled when life turns frantic. You can do this with coffee, tea, soup, or air after rain; whiskey just happens to be a richly layered teacher when handled with care. Try a simple drill: • Aroma Trio: before the first sip, write three precise words. "Sweet" doesn't count; "baked apple," "almond," "clove" do. • Texture Check: thin, oily, silky, drying—choose one. • Finish Map: short, medium, long—where does it live (tongue, cheeks, chest)?

• Compare to a memory (not a review): "Like the cedar closet at the old house." Memory makes tasting human, not competitive. The point isn't to become a critic; it's to strengthen your attention span in a world that keeps trying to saw it into pieces. HYDRATION HABITS (THE "WATER LADDER") A lot of the hidden upside of a whiskey ritual is really a water ritual in disguise. Build a

Water Ladder: • Rung 1: Drink water before you pour. • Rung 2: Keep water within reach of your glass, not across the room. • Rung 3: Take a small sip of water after each nosing round or two small sips. • Rung 4: Finish with water, brush teeth later, sleep better now. Water resets the palate, slows the pace, and reduces the temptation to chase proof with more proof. It also makes mornings boring in the best sense. DIGESTIVE COMFORT, MINUS THE MYTHS There's a romantic story that a dram after dinner "helps digestion." What can we say without pretending whiskey is a tonic? Small sips taken slowly can pair pleasantly with rich meals; the warmth can feel comforting; and the act of lingering at the table encourages conversation instead of overeating. That's a social-behavior benefit, not a medical claim. If your body tells you that even a small pour late at night disrupts your sleep or aggravates your stomach, trust your body and skip it. SLEEP: PROTECT THE NIGHT Alcohol can make you drowsy, but deeper sleep usually prefers a clear system. If you enjoy whiskey, keep timing on your side: • Finish the pour at least three hours before bed. • Use water and a light snack to change gears afterward. • If you track sleep and notice worsened rest, move the ritual earlier or take the night off. • No "nightcap" as a sleep strategy—the next morning sends the bill. CALORIES WITHOUT SURPRISES Whiskey neat carries calories; what it doesn't carry is sugar when unflavored and unsweetened. That doesn't make it "diet." It makes it predictable. You can plan your week accordingly: • Know your pour. Measure a real ounce at home until your eye learns honesty. • Skip mixers when you're not in the mood for extra sugar. • Balance with movement and off days. Pleasure is easier to keep when it has room. OAK, GRAIN, AND "GOOD MOLECULES" (KEEPING IT HONEST) You will hear that whiskey contains antioxidant compounds that come from grain and from the oak. That's true in the same way that a pinch of salt contains minerals—it does, but you shouldn't rely on it as your source. Consider any such compounds an interesting footnote, not a reason to pour more. Let fruit, vegetables, tea, and good sleep do the heavy lifting. Let whiskey do the storytelling. THE BLUE-COLLAR APPROACH TO GLASSWARE AND DILUTION You don't need a museum shelf to taste well. A simple Glencairn or tulip glass concentrates aromas. A small pitcher or eyedropper lets you test dilution without drowning the spirit. Think like a mechanic: small adjustments reveal the engine. Two or three drops can unlock hidden notes; five or six can turn a hot 114 proof into a relaxed 100 that's more enjoyable at a modest pour. Your goal is not to "tame" whiskey; it's to tune it to your night so the night stays good.

A RESPONSIBLE WEEK: THE "TWO-NIGHT, TWO-RULE" PLAN You can enjoy whiskey more by deciding in advance when you will not. Try this simple framework: • Two nights a week for tasting (move them when life demands). • Two rules every time: small pour, early finish. On tasting nights, choose curiosity over collection—explore a new distillery profile, compare different barrel finishes, or revisit a humble bottle that tastes better than the hype said it should. On non-tasting nights, keep the ritual without the ethanol: water in the same glass, tea in the same chair, the same conversation. Consistency keeps the benefits; abstaining keeps the clarity.

BYOB WITH BRAINS: CONTROLLING PROOF AND POUR If your lounge is BYOB, the hidden contribution is control. You choose the proof, the bottle, the amount, and the timing. Harness that: • Bring lower-proof options when you want a longer conversation. • Carry a small flask rather than a full bottle if you're prone to over-sharing. • Place water in front of the whiskey on the table—your hand will find it first. • If people ask for a taste, pour half-ounce splashes into small cups. Celebration does not require weight. BREATHING, POSTURE, AND THE SLOW HAND Whiskey invites a different tempo. Nosing requires slow breaths through the nose and out through the mouth; tasting requires a calm jaw and an easy tongue; sitting well keeps the chest open. These small physical habits counter the hunched, hurried posture of the day. Try "sip posture": both feet on the floor, shoulders down, jaw unclenched, tongue resting. It looks like nothing. After one hour, it feels like something. HOW WHISKEY PULLS CONVERSATION FORWARD (AND WHY THAT HELPS) The glass offers topics that are not work and not politics. "What are you getting on the nose?" can turn into a childhood memory and then into a story that would not have appeared if you'd started with "How's the job?" The structure of tasting—observe, name, compare—teaches people to listen, pause, and respond rather than react. Many of the gains people attribute to "stress relief" come from this shift in conversational style: slower, kinder, more observant. A PRACTICAL PAIRING WITH FOOD THAT RESPECTS THE BODY Food changes how spirits hit you. Plan pairings with respect for your body, not Instagram: • Lean protein before the pour (eggs, chicken, beans). • Something crunchy and neutral during (nuts, crackers). • Avoid very sweet desserts if you want to keep flavors clear. • Finish with water and a walk if weather allows. These aren't "rules." They're field notes from nights that ended well. WHISKEY WITHOUT THE BUZZ (KEEP THE RITUAL ON OFF NIGHTS) You can keep 90% of whiskey's hidden contributions with 0% ethanol. Substitutes for off nights: • Cold black tea with a few drops of vanilla and a shake of bitters in a Glencairn. • Toasted barley tea (mugicha) served neat. • Zero-proof "whiskey-style" mixers diluted heavily—use for aroma and ritual, not for imitation. • Club soda over ice with a twist of orange peel and three shakes of aromatic bitters. Your nervous system learns to relax on cue; chemistry becomes optional.

THE MICRO-SKILLS THAT MAKE A MACRO DIFFERENCE • Pre-commitment: state your end time out loud when you sit. • First-pour patience: nose three times before the first sip. • Drop test: add two drops of water, stir, and re-nose before adding more. • Glass reset: rinse the glass after the last sip, then fill it with water and drink it before you leave. • Courtesy close: thank the host, clean your spot, and step out while the tone is still warm. Each one sounds small. Together they add up to a night you recognize as yours. THE QUIET CONFIDENCE OF SAYING "ENOUGH" One of the healthiest sentences in the whiskey world has only one word: "Enough." Enough to taste complexity. Enough to relax without losing the thread. Enough to leave rather than to finish the bottle. "Enough" respects tomorrow and deepens tonight. The skill is emotional, not chemical: choosing satisfaction over more. PERSONAL POLICY (WRITE IT ONCE; REVISIT OFTEN) A written policy turns an intention into a habit.

Keep it simple: 1) **Why I enjoy whiskey:** flavor, company, a protected hour. 2) **How I protect it:** small pours, water, early finish, dry days. 3) **Where I stop:** ride plan, curfew, no drinks when I'm stressed enough to chase numbness. Read it once a month. Edit when seasons change. Your policy is a fence you build so you don't have to carry a leash. RED FLAGS THAT MEAN "TAKE A BREAK" • You're pouring to change your mood fast rather than to enjoy flavor slow. • You're drinking alone more than you planned and skipping the conversations that used to help. • Sleep is consistently worse on tasting nights even with early finishes. • Friends or family look worried. • A prescription, a condition, or pregnancy makes alcohol a no-go. If any of these ring familiar, switch to the ritual without the ethanol and talk with a professional you trust. There is no loss in choosing clarity. A SIMPLE SELF-AUDIT (WEEKLY) On one page, keep the following boxes and check them on Sundays: • Nights enjoyed with a small pour: • **Dry nights kept:** • Water ladder followed (before/during/after): ☐ ☐ ☐ • End times honored: / • Sleep quality the morning after (worse/same/better): • **Conversations I remember clearly:** • Money spent (planned/unplanned): __ • Notes for next week (move a tasting night? change proof? invite a friend?): This is not for guilt. It's for pattern awareness. Awareness is the lever that moves behavior with the least effort. THE "FIRST DROP" EXPERIMENT (FOR PEOPLE WHO LIKE PROOF) High-proof whiskey is everywhere. If you enjoy it, here's a way to keep the benefit and lose the bite: • Pour a half-ounce into two glasses.

• Add a single drop of water to one and swirl. Nose both. • Add two more drops to the same glass; nose again. • Choose the point where aromas open without collapsing into sweetness. That's your proof for the night. This experiment slows you down, teaches you your preferences, and helps you enjoy less, more. WHY CLEANUP

MATTERS MORE THAN YOU THINK Rinsing your glass, wiping the table, and resetting the chair do more than please the host. They signal to your brain that the ritual is complete, which lowers the urge to "cap" the night with a second pour at home. Endings you can feel prevent beginnings you regret. THE ECONOMY OF ENJOYMENT Keeping pours small, pacing slow, and nights finite is also good for your wallet. A bottle that supports twenty mindful nights does more work than one that fuels four. Buy with intention; price isn't virtue, but scarcity chases people faster than flavor. Keep a house bottle that is always good enough for company and a curiosity bottle that you open when you have time and calm attention. Collect moments, not labels. PAIRING WITH CIGARS WITHOUT OVERDOING EITHER You don't need to pair every time. When you do, pick the leader: • If the cigar is the star, choose a softer whiskey with a clean finish so spice and smoke stay articulate. • If the whiskey is the star, pick a cigar with balance and fewer sharp edges—something that won't turn the finish bitter. • Keep pours extra-small when pairing; the cigar already lengthens the hour. • Water earns its seat more during pairings—more complexity means more resets. The goal is mutual respect, not mutual escalation. HUMILITY AS A HEALTH MECHANIC We don't usually list humility in a chapter like this, but it belongs. Humility keeps the ritual small, keeps you teachable, lets you skip a night without a speech, and allows you to hear when someone who loves you says, "You seem off—everything okay?" Pride reaches for more; humility reaches for water. Pride pretends; humility adjusts. In long, ordinary lives, humility is a powerful health tool. SEASONAL STRATEGIES • **Summer:** heat magnifies effect. Cut proof, cut pour, add water. Patio nights mean sunscreen, shade, and extra politeness to neighbors with open windows. • **Autumn:** richer meals invite richer whiskeys—counter with slower pacing and earlier finish times. • **Winter:** cold amplifies the warmth of spirits; don't let that encourage second pours. Hot tea before bed beats a "nightcap." • **Spring:** a good season for inventory—gift or trade bottles you're not reaching for; tighten your plan before summer weekends try to blow it up. TEN SENTENCES TO LIVE BY (WHISKEY EDITION) 1) Small pours make big memories. 2) Water in reach, car out of the plan. 3) The glass is a teacher, not a dare. 4) Proof is interesting; pace is everything. 5) If sleep suffers, move the ritual or skip it. 6) Share in sips; generosity is attention, not volume. 7) Curiosity tastes better than status. 8) Clean spot, clean exit, clean conscience. 9) Keep more dry days than you think you need.

10) "Enough" is the best toast to tomorrow. WHY THIS CHAPTER EXISTS Someone will ask why a book about whiskey and cigars would bother to talk about "health" at all. Because adults deserve full context. The same honesty that names risk can also name the

quiet, ordinary ways a ritual improves life when it is kept small, slow, and social—lower stress through breathing and pacing, stronger friendships through steady presence, clearer attention through sensory training, better mornings through water and curfews, calmer finances through modesty, and a reputation for responsibility that keeps lounges open and families at ease. CLOSING: KEEP WHAT'S GOOD, SHRINK WHAT ISN'T The hidden contributions of whiskey are not hiding in the bottle. They're hiding in how you use it: a small glass that signals "slow down," a circle of people that reminds you that you matter, a set of habits that chooses tomorrow while you still have tonight. Keep what's good. Shrink what isn't. When in doubt, pour less, talk more, and leave early with the key still in your pocket—the key that locks in all the benefits we're actually after: presence, connection, clarity, and the simple pride of self-control that lasts

longer than any finish.

CHAPTER 11

The Future of the Lifestyle

The culture around whiskey and cigars has always been a conversation between past and present. Oak and leaf are old; how we gather around them is new every year. This chapter looks forward without forgetting what brought us here: moderation, manners, craftsmanship, and community. The future won't be decided by algorithms or press releases; it will be decided one small habit at a time—how we treat each other in lounges, how we buy, how we store, how we talk in public, how we leave a sidewalk at close. Here is a practical map for keeping what's good while adapting to what's coming. A QUIET THESIS The lifestyle will thrive where three things overlap: adult responsibility, honest craft, and welcoming rooms. Responsibility keeps doors open. Craft keeps people interested. Welcome keeps them coming back. When one leg shrinks, the stool wobbles. The future is not a new trick; it is a thousand small, boring decisions that protect those three legs. TRENDS YOU CAN ACTUALLY FEEL (NOT

JUST READ ABOUT) • Broader participation. More women, more couples, more first-time adults who value experiences over collections. • BYOB and hybrid models. Shops that offer retail, lockers, and bring-your-own beverages, plus better non-alcohol options. • Value focus. People want excellence at working-person prices; house blends and store picks will matter more. • Education over hype. Tasting nights, "how to humidor" clinics, and friendly mentorship beat limited-release stampedes. • Outdoor and airflow design. Patios, better ventilation, and sound control will separate thriving lounges from fading ones. THE SOCIAL CONTRACT, UPDATED BUT FAMILIAR Rules that carried us this far will carry us further: be an adult about alcohol, be kind about smoke, be clean about space, be clear about consent (photos, posting, tagging), be generous in tasters not torrents, be early in goodbyes. The update is that these norms must be posted and practiced, not assumed. Newcomers won't guess our standards; they'll copy what they see. The rooms that model good endings will own the future. AIR, LIGHT, AND SOUND: THE NEW "COMFORT TRIANGLE" Tomorrow's great lounges will be designed around three things people feel before they notice décor:

Airflow: fresh air cycles, directional ventilation to keep smoke moving, filters changed on schedule. • **Light:** warm, indirect light that flatters human faces and lets you read a band without squinting. • **Sound:** soft surfaces and placement that allow conversation at normal volume even when the room is full. If you're a customer, support shops that invest here. If you help run a lounge, these upgrades are marketing you can't photograph but everyone remembers. THE HUMIDOR, FUTURE-PROOFED One well-run walk-in can handle more traffic than two neglected ones. Expect more shops to adopt: • Digital hygrometers with remote alerts, but analog backups for when batteries die. • Zoning: slightly different humidity for delicate Connecticuts versus thick, oily maduros—achieved with airflow, not drama. • Clear labeling that teaches: country, wrapper-binder-filler, strength, flavor hints, rolling date if available. • "Candy Store" order without the chaos: new arrivals grouped sensibly, value shelves obvious, staff favorite tags honest. • Locker policies that include a cleanliness clause: tidy boxes, no food in lockers, rotation to prevent forgotten stock from aging into mulch.

SUSTAINABILITY WITHOUT SLOGANS Expect more questions about where wood and water come from. Sensible answers beat slogans. • Cedar & boxes: shops can prioritize suppliers using responsibly sourced wood and lighten waste by recycling or repurposing boxes. • Bags & bands: paper over plastic when feasible; minimal packaging where possible. • Whiskey side: lighter bottles, transparent sourcing, water stewardship at the distillery. • Personal practice: buy what you will enjoy within its ideal window; storage without hoarding is the greenest habit of all.

INCLUSION AS A HABIT, NOT A CAMPAIGN The healthiest rooms feel like family in the best sense: the table grows when a new cousin shows up. What that looks like tomorrow: • Greetings for everyone, not just familiar faces. • No gatekeeping jokes about who "belongs." • Events that welcome different palates (mild-to-medium flights, non-alcohol pairings, coffee and tea nights). • Clear processes for handling discomfort: if someone is treated poorly, staff respond immediately and directly. • Photo consent as a posted rule. The future belongs to shops that protect privacy and welcome diversity without turning either into a performance. ZERO-PROOF AND LOW-PROOF OPTIONS (A PERMANENT SEAT AT THE TABLE) Adult doesn't mean ethanol. Expect better zero-proof choices, not as scolding replacements but as honorable partners: club soda with bitters, high-quality teas, cold brew, and grown-up mixers that don't taste like candy. Pairings can include aromas and textures that flatter cigars without pushing proof—ginger, citrus oils, roasted barley tea, lightly sweetened tonic. The message to members: your seat at the table isn't rented by ABV. THE NEW ETIQUETTE OF PHONES Phones are part of the future; etiquette keeps them from owning the room. • Silent by default; calls taken outside. • Photos only with permission; never film someone without asking. • No speakerphone, ever. • If you're posting a shop moment, tag with consent and show the place at its best: clean tables, happy faces, no bottles in laps, no ashes on floors.

This is not fussy. It's how a room tells the wider world, "We know how to behave." ADVOCACY THAT ACTUALLY WORKS Public policy changes shaped this culture before and will again. The rooms that survive will cultivate advocates who sound like neighbors, not defendants. • Talk specific use patterns: adult-only rooms, occasional use, non-inhalation typicality, ventilation standards. • Offer responsible commitments: ID checks, posted rules, cleanup protocols, ride support. • Build relationships with nearby businesses; invite them to concerns meetings twice a year. • Sweep your sidewalk nightly. Cleanliness removes talking points from critics more effectively than any thread online. THE ECONOMY OF TASTE: HOW TO KEEP IT AFFORDABLE Inflation and taxes push prices. Value is the future. Practical strategies: • Keep a "core five" list of honest, everyday sticks you buy repeatedly. • Split boxes with friends; trade singles to explore without bloating your stash. • Treat limited editions as dessert, not dinner. • For whiskey: buy bottles that shorten the distance between cost and joy; chase flavor, not scarcity. • Host "brown-bag nights" where everyone brings a blind pour or an unbanded stick with a $ limit. Discovery without hierarchy keeps rooms humble. EDUCATION AS A SUPERPOWER Nothing resists fads like knowledge. Expect more: • Humidor 101 sessions (cut, light, storage, ash etiquette). • Palate workshops: side-by-side wrappers; the same whiskey proofed down in small steps; simple tools (water droppers, aroma jars). • "New to the room?" welcome cards: where the fridge is, where glasses are stored, how cleanup works, how to ask for a ride. A culture that teaches becomes a culture that lasts. SAFETY BUILT IN, NOT TACKED ON The future audience expects safety as part of hospitality. • Rides: QR codes on tables linking to rideshare; a sign that says "Ask us—we'll help." • Heat & weather plans for patios; shade and water visible on hot days. • Clear off-ramps: staff trained to suggest water and gently cut off alcohol service in BYOB settings when needed. • Allergy and sensitivity awareness: air purifiers maintained; doors closed; respectful handling of non-smoking areas. TECH WILL HELP, BUT BEWARE THE GIMMICKS Useful tech: digital locker management, text alerts for events, humidity sensors with alarms, POS systems that remember favorite blends (with consent). Gimmicks: flavor "AI generators" that spit out tasting notes nobody actually tastes, or gadgets that complicate simple tasks. The rule for tech is the same as for pairings: if it makes the hour calmer and kinder, keep it. If it adds noise, pass. THE RISE OF HOUSE BLENDS AND STORE PICKS Expect more shops to work with factories and farms for honest, distinctive blends under their banner. Done right, house cigars can be priced fairly and built to match local palates. Similarly, store-pick whiskey barrels—when selected by people with taste and humility—let a shop offer something that reflects the room. The key is

transparency: where it was made, what it is, why it tastes the way it does. Hype fades; clarity sticks. WORLD WHISKEY AND NEW LEAF REGIONS The map is bigger than it used to be. You'll see more excellent whiskey from places that weren't on your shelf a decade ago, and more leaf from regions refining their voice. Approach with curiosity and the same moderation rules as ever. If you treat new origins like teachers rather than trophies, the room grows wiser without growing snobbier. THE ART OF SMALL EVENTS Tomorrow's best gatherings will be smaller, smarter, and more frequent. • Theme nights that teach (wrapper flights, proof ladders, blender Q&A by video). • Charitable tie-ins—with receipts and results published—because generosity feels better when it's accountable. • Quiet hours: posted windows where screens are off and conversation leads. • Early endings on weeknights that everyone honors. Small events create rhythm. Rhythm beats spectacle. THE CARD TABLE AND THE QUIET CHAIR Spaces work best when they acknowledge different speeds. Not every member wants cards or a game; not every member wants a solemn hush. The future is zoning: card table over here, conversation cluster there, the TV corner far enough away that sports don't drown sentences. Respect flows from design before it flows from reminders. COLLECTIONS

RIGHT-SIZED FOR REAL LIFE Most of us don't need a museum at home—just a working library. • Keep a shelf for "tonight," a drawer for "next month," and a small box for "special." • Rotate inventory so nothing forgets why you bought it. • For whiskey, log open dates; oxygen does work, and not always the kind you want. • Share what you're not reaching for. Generosity clears space and builds friendships. PUBLIC FACING, PRIVATE MINDED Social media isn't going away. Use it well. • Post moments that represent the values of the room: clean, calm, kind. • Praise staff publicly; give feedback privately. • When you see misinformation, answer with patience or not at all. Not every post needs your hour. BUILDING THE NEXT GENERATION OF STEWARDS Legacy is not about hoarding rare bands; it's about handing down good habits. • Invite newcomers to make the first cut—teach, don't perform. • Explain the why behind rules: not "don't," but "here's how we keep this room good." • Rotate small leadership tasks: cleanup captain, water restock, humidor tidying, event setup. Ownership turns customers into caretakers. RIDING THE REGULATORY WAVES Policies will shift. Rooms survive by staying nimble: • Keep a compliance binder: ventilation maintenance, ID training, incident logs, neighbor communications. • Maintain relationships with city staff; be the shop that solves problems before others complain. • Be ready to move more enjoyment outdoors in temperate months; invest in heaters or shades that are safe and quiet.

• Treat changes as a chance to showcase maturity, not a stage for outrage. THE HEALTH CONVERSATION, KEPT ADULT We don't run from risk or romanticize it. We keep the moderation code visible, we discourage inhalation, we keep water and zero-proof options plentiful, we encourage rides, and we insist that anyone with a medical or personal reason to abstain feels entirely welcome. That posture will matter more, not less, in the years ahead. TEN-YEAR LOUNGE BLUEPRINT (SHORT VERSION) 1) Invest in air, light, sound. 2) Post clear, kind rules. 3) Train staff in hospitality and de-escalation. 4) Keep a stocked water and zero-proof station. 5) Run small, educational events monthly. 6) Maintain neighbor relationships with scheduled touchpoints. 7) Audit humidor and lockers quarterly. 8) Make inclusion a behavior, not a banner. 9) Build an advocacy team that speaks calmly and cleans sidewalks. 10) Celebrate good endings—say it out loud at close. PERSONAL FUTURE-PROOF CHECKLIST • I keep a two-night plan and dry days. • I bring water, pour small, and leave early. • I greet newcomers and show them the ropes. • I spend most of my money on what I actually enjoy, not what I'm told to enjoy. • I learn one new thing a month—about leaf, whiskey, or hospitality. • I clean my spot and thank the host. • I separate the ritual from ethanol when I want clarity. • I ask for consent before photos and give it only when I mean it. • I correct myths with patience or I let them pass. • I remember that the point is people. WHY THIS STILL FEELS BLUE-COLLAR Because the best parts are earned, not purchased: steady manners, careful pours, a chair offered to someone new, a ride given without announcement, a fridge stocked with water in the next room, a table wiped, a lighter returned, a laugh that doesn't need to be the loudest to be the best. The future respects those fundamentals more than ever. Gadgets will change; headlines will flare and fade. Oak, leaf, and human decency will remain. CLOSING: KEEP THE DOORS OPEN If tomorrow's rooms are going to be as good as the ones that made us fall in love with this lifestyle, we'll have to build them—one welcome, one pour, one clean table, one measured puff at a time. The future is not far away; it is the next hour you spend with people you respect. Keep it adult, keep it kind, keep it small enough to leave something great for next time. That's how the lifestyle not only survives, but improves.

CHAPTER 12

Closing Thoughts: A Blue Collar Philosophy

A blue-collar philosophy isn't a slogan. It's a way of carrying yourself when no one's grading and everyone's watching. It's work boots under the table and a clean ashtray when you stand. It's the habit of leaving a room better than you found it, of pouring small because you plan to come back, of greeting the next person through the door like you already know you'll like them. If this book has tried to say one thing, it's this: the good life around whiskey and cigars isn't about collecting bottles or bands. It's about the kind of person you become by practicing small, steady manners in the company of other adults.

Every lounge is different. The one I favor isn't mine —it's just my favorite place. The chairs there are real leather, not recliners, set up in clusters so conversation doesn't have to shout. Some nights a few of the guys pull a chair to the card table and work the same friendly argument with a deck. Down the hall there's a room with the fridge: water, soda, sometimes a beer, and a K-cup machine that hums like an old friend. It's BYOB, and if there's something in the fridge, you help yourself like you would at a cousin's house. You rinse the cup you used, you throw away your trash, and you clean up any mess you made. No one has to say it. We all learned it the first week. The humidor—one big walk-in—is often called the Candy Store. Not everyone uses that name, but you hear it often enough. Boxes line both sides, cedar and paper and ink, colors that look like they understand time. You step in and the smell hits you: leaf and wood, humidity and promise. People slow down in there. It's not a place to rush. Someone always holds the door for the next person, and when you're done, you bring the band to the counter like you're introducing a friend. The host and the tobacconist are usually the same person, and their welcome is the best thing in the building. "Glad you're here," they say—and they mean it. A lot of nights someone says "Welcome home," and it lands right in the center of your chest. This place taught me that a blue-collar philosophy is a collection of small habits that add up to dignity. Here are the ones I keep. SHOW UP, AND SHOW UP WELL Some nights you'll stay home. You should. Family and rest matter. But when you do come to the lounge, arrive on purpose. Put your phone on silent before you enter. Bring a modest bottle if you're in the sharing mood, but keep it close so no one feels pressure to pour heavy. Carry your own lighter and cutter. If you need a glass, they're in the room down the hall—get one, use it, wash it, and put it back. You don't need to announce any of that. People notice manners even when they don't mention them. GREET EVERYONE You don't have to know a person to greet them. A nod works. A "How ya doin'?" works. A "You new here? Glad you came by." works even better. This is a family room for grownups, and family starts with a hello. We're equal in here—no one cares what you do for a living, what you look like, who you pray to, or how you vote. If the room means anything, it means everyone gets a chair. POUR SMALL, TALK LONG Nothing ruins a good night like a heavy hand. We learned that early. Start with a small pour. If it's high proof, add a drop or two of water and watch the whiskey open up like a window. Switch to soda or water if your conversation gets better than the pour deserves. When the talk is the star, the glass is supporting cast. If the glass becomes the star, the talk usually falls apart. SMOKE WITH PATIENCE A cigar is a metronome. It marks the pace of the hour. Slow puffs keep the burn even and the flavors honest. If the ash grows long and symmetrical, you're paying attention. If it turns ragged and the ember tunnels, you're rushing or you're distracted. You can fix both. Let the cigar rest. Let yourself rest. Your night will straighten. KEEP WATER CLOSE The water rule is simple: if you can reach it without thinking, you'll drink it. Put a bottle on the table in front of your glass. Take small sips like you're reminding your body you plan to treat it kindly tomorrow. The best hosts never ask if you want water; they make sure you have it. The best guests never leave a table without refilling the bottle for whoever sits down next. RESPECT THE CANDY STORE The humidor deserves reverence without ceremony. Don't touch the leaf if you don't need to. Don't tap bands on the boxes. Don't block the aisle while you tell a story to someone who hasn't chosen yet. When in doubt, ask the tobacconist. That person has seen a thousand nights and knows which stick belongs to yours. Say thank you. Buy

with joy. And if you find something that sings, tell the next person in line. The room grows wiser when we share what we actually enjoy instead of what we think we're supposed to enjoy. INVITE WITHOUT PUSHING Generosity is part of the culture, but there's an art to it. Offer a taste, not a refill. Hand someone a half-ounce so they can meet a new bottle without making a commitment. If the answer is no, thank them for listening and move on.

We don't label bottles here. They sit next to their owner, and nobody needs a reminder whose is whose. Respect is stronger than a Sharpie. CLEAN UP LIKE YOU'RE AT HOME Blue-collar philosophy shines brightest five minutes before you leave. Knock your ash into the tray, not the floor. Rinse the cup you used and return it to its shelf. Wipe your table's ring with a napkin. Push the chair back in for the next person. It's not about being tidy so the host doesn't yell. It's about finishing well. Endings teach the room more than any speech. LEARN, THEN TEACH, THEN LEARN AGAIN We're all apprentices and teachers in the same hour. The man who shows you how to light carefully might ask you the next week why his cigar keeps canoeing. The woman who knows how to proof down a barrel-strength bourbon might ask you to help pick a mild cigar for her friend who's new. Knowledge circulates. The rule of thumb is simple: don't perform. Help. Ask why before you explain how. If someone wants a quick answer, give them one. If they want a lesson, offer it. If they want quiet, step away and let the room do the teaching. KEEP IT ADULT This room is for grownups. That means ID rules without drama, language that stays decent even when the game on TV doesn't, and jokes that don't make anyone feel like they don't belong. It means declining to post pictures of people who didn't say yes, and never putting someone online who might not want the world to know where they were on a Tuesday. It means arguing about taste—wrapper, region, rye versus malt—while remembering that we don't argue about people. HONOR THE CURFEW The good night ends before the story needs an apology. Say your last light early. On weeknights pick a time and tell someone. When the reminder buzzes, do the kindest thing you can do for your future self: finish the thought, finish the sip, and go. A firm goodbye is the most underrated luxury in the room. It proves you own the night and the night doesn't own you. WELCOME HOME "Welcome home" only works if the room feels like home. That takes intention. The tobacconist in our place watches the door the way a good host watches a driveway. The regulars split their attention between their circle and the person who just stepped in. New faces get a smile, a little tour—here's the humidor, here's the room down the hall with the drinks, water's free, help yourself, glasses are down there too—and a promise that no one will rush them through a choice. Ten minutes later they're part of the place. A month later it's their favorite place too. KEEP YOUR BLUEPRINT SIMPLE When you peel back all the chapters, the blueprint is short:

• People first, always. • Moderation as the operating system. • Craft as the curriculum. • Courtesy as the language. • Cleanliness as the closing prayer. This isn't complicated, but it does require repetition. That's why we write it down.

A NOTE ON EQUALITY Our room proves, over and over, that people who wouldn't end up at the same dinner table anywhere else can share a table here. Tradesmen and teachers, surgeons and sales reps, old, young, black, brown, pale, tattooed, churchgoing, not— everyone takes the same breath when the cedar door swings open. Legends get made one small kindness at a time. Someone gives up a chair. Someone replaces the water jug without being asked. Someone remembers a name. You can't fake that. You can only live it until it becomes the air in the room. THE DIFFERENCE BETWEEN PRICE AND VALUE Price is a number. Value is a night. Blue-collar philosophy buys what tastes good and shares what tastes better. It keeps a short list of honest, dependable sticks that never miss. It buys the occasional surprise and opens it when there's time to pay attention. On the whiskey shelf, it favors bottles you can find again. Rarity is fine; repeatability is better. If a pour makes the conversation better, it was worth it. If it made the conversation disappear, it wasn't. WHY THE RITUAL WORKS The ritual is simple: you slow down on purpose and you pay attention to something that doesn't demand anything loud from you. You cut clean, light carefully, nose the glass, sip without racing, listen more than you talk, and go home with enough left of yourself to be useful in the morning. That's not complicated. It's also not common. In a world that monetizes hurry, a room that runs on patience feels like mercy. TEN LINES TO LIVE BY (FINAL CUT) 1) Small pours, slow puffs, early goodbyes. 2) Water within reach, car out of the plan. 3) Greet first; teach second; clean always. 4) Buy for flavor, not for applause. 5) The humidor is a library—treat the books kindly. 6) Minds open faster than bottles. 7) If the room is family, behave like it. 8) The best story is the one you remember clearly tomorrow. 9) Be the reason someone says, "I felt welcome." 10) Leave a little good in the glass for next time. PASSING IT ON If you care about this lifestyle, you'll leave it better than you found it by turning courtesy into tradition. Bring a newcomer. Show them the door to the Candy Store. Explain humidors without lecturing. Let them choose what they want, not what you want for them. Offer a small pour. Teach them to proof down without drowning. Demonstrate how to ash gently and when to set the cigar down so it doesn't overheat. Tell them the cleanup rules—the ones that live on the wall and the ones that live in the heart: be kind, be clean, be on time, be safe. Give them your chair when you leave. That's how the next generation learns the music. WHAT WE OWE THE NEIGHBORHOOD The room doesn't exist on an island. It has neighbors with kids and customers and opinions. A blue-collar philosophy takes that seriously. It parks where it should. It keeps voices low outside after dark. It doesn't ash on the sidewalk or balance bottles on the curb. It notices the person passing by and steps aside without attitude. It understands that respect outside the door is what lets the door stay open. WHY WE KEEP COMING BACK We come back for the same reason people return to barbershops and porches and church basements and family tables. We come back for the feeling that time can be held in place long enough to mean something. We come back because the chair fits and the voices are familiar and the work of the week slows to a walk. We come back because the room keeps its promises: you'll be welcomed; you'll be safe; you'll be treated like an equal; and you'll leave with something better than you brought in—maybe a flavor you didn't have words for yet, maybe a laugh you

needed more than you knew, maybe the quiet you couldn't find anywhere else. A BENCHMARK FOR YOURSELF Not every night will be perfect. A good baseline helps. Before you step inside, ask three questions: • Can I leave on time? • Can I keep my pour small? • Can I make someone else's night better? If the answers are yes, you're ready. If one is no, choose water and conversation. If two are no, save the cigar and the pour for a better night.

That's not a loss. It's craft. THE WORK AHEAD The future will keep testing us—regulations, prices, public scrutiny, distractions. Our response can be quiet and effective. Keep showing that adult spaces can police themselves. Keep proving that moderation is not a buzzkill but a style. Keep inviting people who don't look or think like you into your circle and treating them like family the second they sit down. Keep saying "welcome home" and meaning it. ONE LAST WALK THROUGH THE ROOM When the hour ends, stand and take a slow glance around. The ashtray is clean. The table is dry. The bottle is where it belongs. The chair is set for the next person. The humidor door is closed behind someone considering a box. Two friends at the card table are arguing softly about a play that doesn't matter and means everything. Someone laughs from the far corner, the sound of a load set down. You nod to the tobacconist—host, referee, teacher, friend—and you mean it when you say, "Thanks." You step into the hallway, return the clean glass to its shelf, and take a last pull of water for the road. Outside the sky is ordinary and perfect. You head home easy, with tomorrow intact. If this lifestyle has given you anything, let it be this: the knowledge that small, careful pleasures practiced with good people can shape a life that fits. You don't need to win the room. You just need to honor it. Carry that with you. Bring it back. End early while the song is still playing. And when the cedar door swings open next time and someone says, "Welcome home," let it be true—because you made it that way. That's the whole philosophy: be grateful, be decent, be steady. The rest is smoke and oak and conversation—the oldest technologies in the world for teaching us how to be human together.

Final Word from the Author

As I set down my pen and the last ember fades, I'm reminded once again that whiskey and cigars are not about indulgence; they are about connection—connection to history, to craft, and to one another. If you've read this far, you've taken a seat beside me in that smoke-filled lounge, and I thank you.

May you always find time to savor the moments, to enjoy the company you keep, and to raise a glass to the simple pleasures that make life rich. Here's to your own stories yet unwritten.

Made in United States
North Haven, CT
17 December 2025

85001365R00139